The Feminine Ideal

PICTURING HISTORY

Series Editors
Peter Burke Sander L. Gilman
Roy Porter Bob Scribner

In the same series

Health and Illness
Images of Difference
Sander L. Gilman

The Devil
A Mask without a Face
Luther Link

Reading Iconotexts
From Swift to the French Revolution
Peter Wagner

Men in Black
John Harvey

Eyes of Love
The Gaze in English and French Paintings
and Novels 1840–1900
Stephen Kern

The Destruction of Art:
Iconoclasm and Vandalism since the French Revolution
Dario Gamboni

Maps and Politics
Jeremy Black

Picturing Empire:
Photography and the Visualization of the British Empire
James Ryan

Trading Territories:
Mapping the Early Modern World
Jerry Brotton

The Feminine Ideal

Marianne Thesander

REAKTION BOOKS

Published by Reaktion Books Ltd
11 Rathbone Place, London W1P 1DE, UK

First published in English 1997

First published in Danish as *Det Kvindelige Ideal* © 1994 Tiderne Skifter

Translated by Nicholas Hills
Designed by Humphrey Stone
Jacket designed by Ron Costley
Photoset by Wilmaset Ltd, Birkenhead, Wirral
Printed and bound in Great Britain by Biddles Ltd,
Guildford and King's Lynn

British Library Cataloguing in Publication Data:
Thesander, Marianne
   The feminine ideal. – (Picturing history)
   1. Lingerie – History 2. Lingerie – Social aspects 3. Body
   image – History 4. Body image – Social aspects 5. Women –
   Identity – History
   I. Title
   391.4′2′09

ISBN 1 86189 004 4

Contents

'Exactly Venus's measurements!' Lithograph, 1830, after Octave Tassert.

Introduction

When she was finally able to go out again, Scarlett had Lou lace her into her stays as tightly as the strings would pull. Then she passed the tape-measure about her waist. Twenty inches! She groaned aloud. That was what having babies did to your figure! Her waist was as large as Aunt Pitty's, as large as Mammy's.

'Pull them tighter, Lou. See if you can't make it eighteen- and-a-half inches or I can't get into any of my dresses.'

'It'll bust de strings,' said Lou. 'Yo' wais' jes' done got bigger, Miss Scarlett, an' dar ain' nuthin' ter do 'bout it.'

Margaret Mitchell, *Gone with the Wind*, 1939

In every society the physical and biological differences between the sexes have formed the basis for images of the ideal female and the ideal male. Both sexes have procreative importance and therefore equal importance as individuals in society, but the ability of women to reproduce has set them apart from men and has been used in varying forms to limit their social and cultural sex roles. And it is this lifegiving ability that has produced a lasting and ambivalent attitude towards the female body: it was regarded as part of nature, with great unknown powers and was, therefore, associated with insecurity and mysticism. Like other areas of nature, too, the female body became the object of social control. The male body, on the other hand, was regarded as both substance and spirit – culture and order – and as an instrument of control.

The female's reproductive function is the deeper reason why she has been accorded a special 'nature', and this in turn has given rise to many myths about the female body. Some of these myths – 'the fair sex', 'the weaker sex', 'the eternal feminine' – are still used to categorize female humanity.

Simone de Beauvoir contested this 'biological ideology' in her major work, *The Second Sex* (1949):

Thus against the dispersed, contingent, and multiple existences of actual women, mythical thought opposes the Eternal Feminine, unique and changeless. If the definition provided for this concept is contradicted by the behaviour of flesh-and-blood women, it is the latter who are wrong: we are told not that Femininity is a false entity, but that the women concerned are not feminine . . .

In actuality, of course, women appear under various aspects; but each of the myths built up around the subject of woman is intended to sum her up *in toto*.[1]

To break the balance of power that makes women into 'Women': that is de Beauvoir's challenge. This may of course sound like a contradiction – for what else can women be if not women? But she believes that female biology has been used to define an eternal and absolute femininity, an image which, in reality, has been created by society and to which women have had to subject themselves if they wanted to be 'real' women.

Her observation 'One is not born a woman – one becomes one' is often quoted. Femininity is not concrete and dependent on biology, but is the product of culture. In order to be accepted as a 'woman' it is not enough to have a woman's body or to be feminine: you have first to meet the social demands of femininity. Such demands are discriminatory and restrictive, partly because they are an obstacle to social equality and partly because they unilaterally attempt to make women fit physically and behaviourally into those feminine ideals that are still being voiced. Nevertheless, these social demands, which have prevailed throughout history, have helped to cast women in the role of aesthetic objects.

This is the situation that Simone de Beauvoir finds objectionable. In her pioneering work she focuses on the right to be counted as an equal human being. She rejects traditional female identity – the 'feminine myth' – and tries to find new ways in which women can become independent and responsible individuals. She herself chose not to have children, a decision which, according to the social norms of the day, was unwomanly, but which according to her was the only solution to the problem. Many other women, both inside and outside the women's movement, have taken up the struggle not to be turned into objects and have tried to reconcile emancipation with a family life and motherhood in different ways. Women's own attitudes towards femininity and their bodies over the last decade have changed fundamentally, particularly because many women have gained greater self-confidence by means of education, work and involvement in decision-making in society, and in so doing have gained a freedom to be women on their own terms.

Femininity is a curiously intangible and fluid term. It is perhaps given its most concrete expression in the construction of feminine ideals and the moulding of the physical form. The body is an organism, but it is also our visible expression in the world and in the culture of which we are part. So the body is well suited to projecting social and cultural meanings; it is both an individual means of expressing ideas and perceptions – about our place in society – and an object formed by society – never quite 'natural', always carrying social and cultural significance. The physical form expresses a relationship both to the individual and to society. In addition, the body is one of the places where the limits between what is morally acceptable and what is not, between the attractive and the repulsive, between liberation and oppression, and so on, are constantly being pushed back.

We exist through our bodies, but it is the formed and moulded body that signals our social position and cultural affiliation. And it is the body as a cultural phenomenon that I shall concentrate on, examining how the 'natural' body, through various artificial means, is re-formed into a cultural image of femininity. This book is about the *production of feminine ideals* and seeks to illuminate how aesthetic ideals are altered and reinterpreted in accordance with prevailing contemporary views on women.

Throughout history, the female body has been the focus of many different interests, to most of which women themselves have had only limited access. Women have been made synonymous with their bodies, the cultural form of which was an expression of the specific meanings that were attached to them. The prevailing perception of the body, of course, also determines the evolution of masculine ideals, but these have not been subject to control in the same way and have therefore not led to the same degree of reshaping of the male body. I focus principally on the feminine ideal, the physical ideal, the alteration of which is closely connected to the changing position of women in society.

Who produces the varying physical expressions? And why is it especially the female body that has, in the course of history, been endowed with specific cultural symbolic significance?

Symbolic communication has played an important role in all societies, but it is especially obvious in many African sculptures. Here, form and function are part of a common unity, and are fundamental and significant elements in a common human concept of life. If not equal to men, women in Africa are highly respected, and motherhood and fertility are fundamental values in African art and culture. African wood figures are seldom anatomically correct representations; rather, the form indicates meanings that have been transferred to the figure. A magic quality is attained by breaking down the body's organic unity and transforming it into something cultural. Certain parts of the body are accentuated, others minimized. For obvious reasons, the breasts are especially accentuated in fertility dolls and motherhood figures. In this way magical powers are transferred to specific parts of the figure by a kind of artifice which is intended to promote fertility, problem-free childbirth and good health.[2]

Female figures with exaggerated and swelling forms symbolizing fertility have been found all over the world. The best-known is the Willendorf Venus, a Paleolithic chalk figure dating from around 21,000 BC. It has enlarged breasts, deformed arms and a featureless head.

Twentieth-century female fertility figure, Côte d'Ivoire. The figure's exaggerated breasts symbolize fertility.

Maternity figure in wood from the Congo. This nursing mother with her baby shows the woman's importance as the source of life.

The Willendorf Venus.

In every culture a female physical ideal is created, by various means of artifice, and given precisely the form and the meanings with which the culture wishes women to be identified. The artificial body can be made the object of symbolic significance; the shape of the body has necessarily to be changed before it can be given new value. Each culture transfers a different significance to the moulded and remodelled body. But whether the social and cultural moulding of the body serves as a ritual, an indicator of status or a fashion symbol, the message is always associated with a physical alteration.

The communicative function is central in the body image – a body language. I approach the present subject from the point of view of cultural communication, with inspiration from semiology, the science that studies the meaning of symbols in social life. I do not intend to attempt a 'pure' semiological analysis such as, for example, Roland Barthes does in *The Fashion System*,[3] but in a modified form to impose symbol analysis on to the changing expression of the physical ideal. Semiology studies all cultural processes as communicative processes, but the cultural phenomena it studies can have functions other than communicative ones: clothes, for example, also have of course a practical function. Culture is thus not purely communication, but it can, as Umberto Eco points out,[4] be better understood from a communicative perspective.

The communicative sign and symbol function is obvious in all cultures as a system of control and interpretation. Like everything else, the body is subject to social control and is given status by being transformed into a cultural ideal, since the dominant class/group in every culture sets the value of the symbols for society as a whole. The ideal of beauty expresses the prevailing aesthetic values, but it is also a visualization of the morality and body image of the dominant class. Their moral concepts become aesthetic as tasteful, agreeable and acceptable – the body is given an aesthetic, narcissistic function. But I would contend that women contribute in various ways to producing female images themselves, both by adjustment to the ideal and by opposition to it. I will try to demonstrate the constant interplay between the commercial female image as a commodity and intermediary of ideals of beauty, and real women as individuals and their physical self-expression. Physical presentation is an expression both of the view a specific period has of women and of the way in which women themselves understand their position in society and their ability to influence this position – self-expression conditioned by the choices available.

This book is divided into two parts. The first part sets out various perspectives on the ideal female body in a broader context across time and space. The second part is an analysis of a concrete process of physical alteration in the period from the 1880s to the 1980s, looking at those elements that shaped the female body so that it approached the prevailing ideal.

THE "SPÉCIALITÉ CORSET."
(Regd.

The Spécialité Corset, from an advertisement of 1901.

Throughout this period the feminine ideal has been altered, but not continuously; various factors provoke change and influence the formation of a new style and new physical ideals in accordance with the spirit of the age and the prevailing physical image. I have divided the hundred-year period into six consecutive periods, each with particular physical characteristics, which both indicate the altered position of women in the family and in society and show how their altered position is reflected in various forms of self-expression. During the period from the 1880s to the 1980s there was an ex-

A new body ideal radiating strength and self-discipline became fashionable in the 1980s.

citing and important change in the position of women in society and in the way in which the process of liberation was reflected in a changing physical expression, either in opposition to the ideal or as an expression of it.

The liberation of women's bodies is closely connected with women's liberation, and for this reason the liberation of the body is highlighted both by the early and the more recent women's movement. A significant part of women's liberation has been the right of a woman to control her own body and her struggle against the powers that continue to maintain women as aesthetic sex objects.

Throughout history, the female body has been shaped to fit in to the prevailing norms of physical aesthetics. In European civilization, the corseted female body has been the most obvious example of a moulded and modified body. The tight-laced corset, which has been in use for close on four hundred years, was the foundation for the changing shape of women's fashionable clothing and a social symbol that showed that one belonged to the privileged classes and did not need to work. But the corset was more than a status symbol: it was a complex of control and meaning systems connected to women's 'frozen' position in society; not surprisingly it was thus regarded as a symbol of women's oppression.

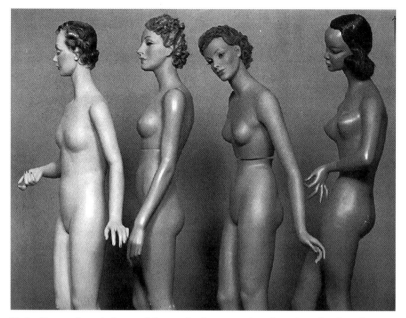

Ideals of beauty through the ages. Mannequins from around 1928, 1936, 1948 and 1956.

As we know, the corset has been largely abandoned. But other forms of corsetry have replaced the corset as a means of controlling the body in this century. Nowadays very few people wear a corset and then it is made of an elastic material so as to make the body look natural, authentic – and yet the naked body is not synonymous with the natural body.

The cult of the body accelerated through the 1980s: whereas before only a few people practised body-building and power training, like any other form of sport and competitive activity – but with the difference that in this case a specific body form was the aim – the cult of the body has spread through nearly all areas of society. All of us are consciously or subconsciously influenced by this idealization of the body, which inevitably alters our perception of what is beautiful and what is ugly.

In Western culture, the cult of the body is widespread: it has become common more or less artificially to 'build up' or 're-create' one's body. Beauty clinics, which offer cosmetic operations to reshape clients' bodies, are frequented not only by models or actresses or others who earn their living by looking good, but also by perfectly ordinary women who, after the operation, say they feel much happier with their 'new body'!

The corset, the bra, the roll-on girdle, body-building and cosmetic surgery are various forms of artifice used to alter the body. Even if the female body has today been liberated from tight and confining corsetry, it has by no means been liberated from idealization and alteration to conform with contemporary perceptions.

The history of the female body is to a great extent about changes in social, cultural and fashion moulding. The last four hundred years of body history are thus also the history of the corset and other items of clothing designed to control the body. But however much the human body is altered and adapted to the ideal, it will never be perfect: only mannequins made of wax or glass fibre have 'perfect' bodies.

The fashionable ideal of the day is not limited to dress alone: it is a question of one's whole appearance and physical expression. Mannequins are naked figures, made to fit in with developments in fashion which determine the proportions, posture and fullness of the body's curves. The figures do not merely represent a female or a male body: they are also, with their moulded, idealized bodies and precisely the right appearance, the manifestations of the ideal contemporary, fashionable image.

PART I THE FEMALE PHYSICAL IDEAL

Padaung girl from Myanmar with brass neck rings.

1 The Status Image

There is no totally natural or neutral body – even the naked body reflects the culture to which it belongs. From birth our bodies are a part of our culture's order. In many cultures bodies are decorated and altered by painting, tattoos, changes to the shape of the head, etc. Thus, even without clothes, the body is equipped with distinctive cultural and social characteristics.

People began to wear clothes for a number of different reasons. The most commonly cited are the protection of the body from the climate, modesty and the symbolic function of clothes. Which of these reasons is taken to be the primary one depends on one's way of looking at the body and clothing. The symbolic function of clothes seems to be the most important reason for the use of costume, whereas the protective function and the demand for decency must be ascribed more to the growth and spread of civilization over time – as anthropological studies have shown.

When in December 1832 Charles Darwin visited Tierra del Fuego (known as the 'country of fire' because of the fires Europeans had seen from their ships, rather than for its climate, which is relatively harsh), he found that the inhabitants were naked, whereas he and his fellow Europeans, though wearing clothes, still froze in the cold. Later he described his encounter with the people:

Amongst these central tribes the men generally have an otter skin, or some small scrap about as large as a pocket-handkerchief, which is barely sufficient to cover their backs as low down as their loins . . . But these Fuegians in the canoe were quite naked, and even one full-grown woman was absolutely so. It was raining heavily, and the fresh water, together with the spray, trickled down her body. In another harbour not far distant, a woman, who was suckling a recently born child, came one day alongside the vessel . . . whilst the sleet fell and thawed on her naked bosom, and on the skin of her naked baby! These poor wretches were stunted in their growth, their hideous faces bedaubed with white paint, their skins filthy and greasy, their hair entangled . . . It was most amusing to see the undisguised smile of satisfaction with which one young woman . . . tied several bits of scarlet cloth round her head with rushes.[1]

Darwin's attitude was typical of his time. The natives' behaviour and nakedness were proof that they were primitives. This view was fully in tune with contemporary ideas of evolution, which held that all societies would undergo the same development from simple, primitive forms to higher, more complex ones. The Fuegians were living proof that the need for clothes for protection of the body against heat and cold is not general. They also demonstrated that their culture was not expressed through clothing. In other cultures, at different times and in different places, the degree to which people cover their bodies and faces with clothes cannot always be interpreted as an expression of modesty but rather of cultural conventions. The need to show status in society – 'who am I?' – and to signal cultural and social affiliation with a particular group and distinctness from another underlies the use of clothes, decoration and physical alteration.

In many so-called primitive cultures tattooing and artificial scarring (scarification) have been practised in connection with initiation rites, marking transitions in life from one role or status to another, 'rites of passage'. Body decoration was an important part of the ritual and symbolized newly acquired status.

The transition for girls happens suddenly with the onset of menstruation, which marks a natural dividing line between girlhood and sexually mature womanhood. But there is no corresponding decisive point at which a boy can say, 'Now I am a man'. Society marks the transition for boys symbolically.[2] In many societies boys have to pass a test of strength and courage and to undergo tattoos, cutting of the skin, body painting or other physical alterations in order to be awarded the status of adult. The transition to adult status also brings with it a greater division between the sexes, with specific sex role functions that illustrate that culture's ideals of the 'masculine' and the 'feminine'. The alteration of the body, the re-creation of nature, is a social sign which also helps to maintain cultural order. This alteration makes bodies into parts of the culture and the social groups within it.

Tattooing is known from as early as the southern French Ice Age caves where the paintings depict naked women with scars across their stomachs.[3] We cannot know what these adornments symbolized; but much more recently in New Guinea and in many places in Africa it was the custom to decorate girls' bodies with tattoos before marriage as a way of trying to endow them with a magical power to ensure fertility.

Fertility has been of extreme importance in nature and society for thousands of years and is, therefore, a recurrent theme in the art of many cultures, of course representing aesthetic values, but first and foremost connected with ritual and magical functions. Fertility in women is, for

(left) Scarification across the stomach of a pregnant woman of the Kalari tribe, Nigeria.

(right) The Japanese art of tattooing on a woman's back.

the most part, represented by female and mother-and-child figures. The woman is defined as a mother: her life is divided into three different stages, based on her ability to give birth, to which different social roles and cultural meanings are attached.[4] Biology has been used socially and culturally to maintain various feminine ideals based exclusively on motherhood. This perception of sex has not generally been used directly as a means of oppression, but by cutting women off from participating in most functions outside the domestic sphere – by not giving women any choice with regard to work – myths of femininity have been perpetuated and have indirectly worked as a mechanism for oppression.

As with other forms of physical alteration, tattooing is used for various reasons, but always in connection with a specific cultural perception of the body and values. In Western cultures, tattooing has been used most often by sailors – more recently also by members of certain male subcultures such as bikers or rockers as a symbol of masculine strength and social group identification. The Japanese very early developed a refined form of tattooing which was confined to the upper classes.

The fact that King Frederik IX of Denmark (1899–1972) was heavily tattooed caused a great deal of surprise, but then he regarded himself as a sailor, after all. In 1951, when photographs of King Frederik were being published around the world, Karen Blixen wrote: 'I put my faith in the art of tattooing. It is a ritual art, a cult. ... Its most important clientele comprised seamen and kings, people who still to this day must have some sense of ritual.'[5]

The Japanese art of tattooing, *irezumi*, is still practised. The entire body is covered with rich ornamentation, forming a kind of ritual clothing. In women it is particularly the back that is transformed into a work of art, presumably because in Japan this part of a woman has always been looked upon as a zone of intense erotic interest.

Interest in body decoration grew in Western countries throughout the 1980s. The post-Modernist expression that achieved increasing importance within the fields of architecture, design and fashion also became important within the area of physical expression as the body itself became increasingly important as a means of communication. The growing cult of the body and an increased interest in the body decoration of other cultures have meant that tattooing and other forms of body decoration have become more widespread among young people. More young girls in the West have flowers, butterflies and other ornaments tattooed on to their bodies but often in less visible places. Most do it because they think it is attractive and interesting and to express their individuality – in a way, the opposite function of body decorations in the cultures from which they have taken their inspiration, where class or group affiliation and status are paramount.

Differences in material circumstances and in social position have been made most obvious in costume and body decoration, both as indicators of status and as a means of control, in that all societies set rules for dress and body decoration.

Ancient Egypt was a class-divided society, as was expressed in clothing conventions, among other things: a slave or servant either went naked or wore a simple loincloth, while an aristocrat wore a loose, decorated robe. This was not worn primarily for protection nor out of modesty – the almost transparent fabric neither retained much heat nor concealed the body effectively – but as a means of underlining the class distinctions in society. Egyptian clothing remained more or less unchanged for around a thousand years – an indication that class divisions did not change very much either. The rich collection of works of art representing slaves, servants, peasants, craftsmen and the aristocracy confirms this.

The ideal woman throughout Egyptian history had a slim figure which was never artificially constricted. On the other hand, the shape of the Pharaohs' heads could not have been achieved without some artificial means.

Bust of Queen Nefertiti, wife of Amenhotep IV (Ekhnaton), who reigned *c.* 1375-58 BC.

The moulded headform of one of Amenhotep IV's daughters, 1360 BC, demonstrating the Egyptian ideal of beauty.

Padaung woman with a number of brass neck, arm and leg rings.

Deformation of the skull has been used in many different cultures as a sign of high social status and as an aesthetic ideal. The shape of the head was altered in ancient Peru by pressing a baby's soft skull between two boards in order to make the forehead flat. In several places in Africa tight bandages have been used to achieve the desired shape. In many of these cultures it was common to carry water jars and other objects on the head: a pointed skull showed that the person belonged to the upper class and was not expected to carry out the usual physical work.

Another form of body deformation is practised by the Padaung of Myanmar (Burma), producing the 'giraffe-necked' effect.[6] From the age of around five, girls begin to wear metal rings around their necks, new rings being added every second year until there are between twenty-two and twenty-four of them. The women are able to carry out work in the fields and in the home with this neck support – which weighs several kilos – but if the neck rings are removed, the neck muscles are no longer able to support the weight of the head and collapse. This punishment is used if a wife is unfaithful. The custom of wearing metal rings around the neck, arms and legs is dying out today but it used to be followed exclusively by Paduang women as a means of marking themselves out from the other Karen peoples.

The Tutsi women of Burundi also used to wear very heavy metal rings on their necks, arms and legs to mark their social position. In other cultures, people have changed the shape of hands and feet or pierced and put rings, discs or pieces of wood or metal into ears, noses or lips. Alterations to the body produce not only an ideal physical image but also an image of status.

In European societies too, body shape has been altered in various ways to make it correspond to the ideal image of beauty. The difference is that, whereas body alteration in more primitive cultures was practised on both sexes, in more sophisticated cultures it has principally been the female body that has been subjected to constant modification.

The corset in European female dress and the 'three-inch golden lotus', as the tightly bound feet of Chinese women were called, are probably the best-known devices for changing the female shape. Both forms of binding reduced women's freedom of movement and marked their unsuitability for work, but in return the women were seen to have high status. In China, the crippled but much-prized small women's feet were a sign of female value and thus important in negotiating a bride price. The feet of girls from wealthy families were tightly bound from the age of about six. A bandage was wound tightly over the four small toes so that they were forced back on themselves. Only the big toe escaped this mutilation. The bandage was then bound round the heel to reduce the distance between the heel and the toes as much as possible. The aim was to reduce the foot to about one third of its natural size. As adults the girls were invalids, although everyone admired them. Because they were unable to work, the women were dependent on their husbands' income and in this way served to enhance their status. The 'golden lotus' disappeared with the Mandarin régime after the revolution of 1911.

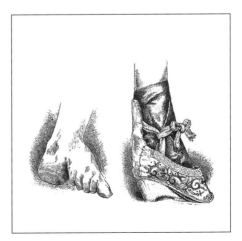

'Three-inch golden lotus' – as the small, mutilated feet of Chinese women were called – were coveted attributes.

'Toilette', showing the corset being tightened by a lady's maid. Etching by Ponce after a drawing by Baudoin, 1771.

Wearing a corset was also a sign of wealth. It demonstrated that one could afford servants to do the housework; and the mere process of tying the laces required the assistance of a lady's maid.

The corset is the single item of European clothing that has had the greatest importance as a basis for women's dress. Introduced as the foundation for fashionable dress, and gaining in popularity between the late Middle Ages and the early Renaissance, the corset acquired social meaning as an expression of upper-class rank. The tightly laced corset was first and foremost a social marker, but it was significant in other respects too.

In his major work *The Theory of the Leisure Class* (1899), Thorstein Veblen took a socio-economic view of the study of the upper classes' methods of demonstrating their wealth.[7] Here, as with many other analyses of material culture, dress plays a central role. It is more visible than any other material cultural product and it is with us wherever we go. So dress is well suited to expressing social status and indicating how the wearer wishes to be regarded by others.

Veblen was an economist, so his thought processes were rational – something that fashion never is. He looked particularly at the status and consumer aspects that characterize fashionable dress, but from a social, cultural and historical perspective. Veblen introduced some important terms – conspicuous consumption and leisure – into his analysis of the demonstrative purpose of clothes among different classes and at different periods. The principle of conspicuous consumption has prevailed throughout history and is still noticeable, although, with time, other ideals have come to the fore as markers of social value.

Veblen looked at that section of society that does not need to work – the unproductive or leisure class – and illuminated the ways in which this class has maintained conspicuous consumption and lifestyle as a means to distance itself from other classes. He pointed out that wealthy women in a patriarchal society dress luxuriously not only because their clothing represents aesthetic value in itself but also because the way they dress makes their husbands' wealth obvious, which is an important adjunct to the husbands' social status. 'Beauty' and 'purpose' thus derive from each other. Of the corset in Europe and the tightly bound feet in China, Veblen wrote that such treatment made women a visible sign of wealth – both 'useless' and 'precious'.

Veblen showed how in different ways the dominant class produces status symbols in order to create social classification. Baudrillard further developed Veblen's theoretical ideas, but using a semiotic perspective to illuminate material culture and consumption. He wrote, 'The "Veblen effect" – "I am buying this because it is more expensive" – is an important aspect in which the economic is converted into sign-difference. In the case of signs, the "Veblen effect" becomes the absolute rule.'[8]

But, whereas Veblen emphasized that the establishment of class differences is the fundamental principle in the creation of material forms of consumption, Baudrillard analyses the production of symbols from the point of view of a so-called political economy, as an ideological social system that produces elements at all levels to become bearers of these ideas. The connection to the system indicates the aesthetic-functional value of the elements and this value changes in accordance with changes in society and the economy. On a more abstract level, the changing aesthetic expression of fashion, according to Baudrillard, can be attributed to this model for the social production of symbols and values.

Baudrillard defines consumption not merely structurally as a system of symbols and their changes, but also as a power strategy. Consumption becomes a system of coded symbols or symbols carrying meaning. He maintains that the status value of things is not the same as their actual practical value. It is not the things themselves that are consumed, but the status value that is ascribed to them when they are made into symbols. Barthes expresses the same point of view in his analysis of the fashion system when he writes that clothes have no special significance until they become attractive as fashion symbols.[9] The body and clothes are transformed into a creation of symbols under social control – social values are ascribed to the body and these change with the dominant social group.

In pre-industrial society the clothes of both sexes in the upper classes were expensively and richly decorated – prestige dress reserved for the privileged, who had no need to work. The French Revolution of 1789 changed the balance of power, politically, economically and socially. With the fall of

The new, simply cut men's clothes of 1838 featured short tailored coats and narrow trousers.

the aristocracy the bourgeoisie became increasingly dominant – a development that also had an influence on dress, especially men's dress. The bourgeois gentleman no longer walked about dressed like a dandy: simplicity and good tailoring became the essential points of his dress. In time, men abandoned decoration on their clothes entirely – a phenomenon Flügel calls 'the great masculine renunciation',[10] whereas women's dress was still an expression of conspicuous consumption and leisure. In the 1800s it was only women who demonstrated their own and their husbands' social position through their dress; an expression of the great inequality between the social roles of men and women that characterized this century.

New economic and social conditions create a need for new modes of expression. After the industrial revolution the perception of the body also changed. It became important for the bourgeoisie to transfer their disciplinarian demands on their bodies to the working classes so that the working classes could labour efficiently and uniformly. Industry demanded a stable workforce, but this was achievable only if the working-class body was able to adjust to the new conditions of production. Industrialization brought alterations to the way of life and new patterns of consumption: this was the start of the modern consumer society. The old status symbols no longer served the purpose of marking social differences and were replaced by new ones.

When most labouring people were employed in agriculture, which involved a lot of outdoor work and made them sunburnt and weather-beaten, a smooth, white skin was an indication of wealth. Even peasant girls tried to keep their skin pale by wearing sunhats, because it was not 'nice' to be sunburnt. But as paid work increasingly became concentrated in the factories and offices of the cities, paleness became commonplace. Particularly after the 1920s a slim, suntanned body became characteristic of the upper classes: it showed that they could afford to take time off, to go on holiday, perhaps abroad, and to get a suntan.

Although it has been proved that too much sunbathing and especially the exaggerated use of solaria increase the risk of skin cancer and that lengthy exposure to the sun's rays will make the skin age more quickly and become leathery, the suntan has remained a sought-after status symbol, reinforced by the growing cult of the body in the 1980s.

The cult of slimness has also accelerated rapidly throughout the twentieth century in Western societies. In cultures where food is in short supply and only the wealthy can afford to satisfy their hunger, plump people are also attractive people. In Western welfare societies, on the other hand, where there is no real shortage of food, the ideal is a slim, supple and youthful body, the attainment of which demands that time and money be spent on body care, exercise and the 'correct' food. This kind of food,

Sun worship. Bathing fashions in *Vogue*, 1930.

(opposite) Leslie Hornby, also known as Twiggy, the English beanpole who became a top model and an idol for many young girls. Her unhealthily thin body could easily be confused with that of an anorexic.

however – lean meat, fish and vegetables, for example – is expensive and not everyone can afford it. Obesity and overweight are regarded as signs of lower social status since only the wealthy can afford to keep themselves slim and fit.

If one looks at slimming propaganda in fashion and women's magazines over the past sixty years, surprisingly little has changed. Both then and now women are told that if they do not do something before the summer to get down to the ideal weight, they can give up any thought of going to the beach: a swimming costume will mercilessly show up any extra kilos. Women's weeklies publish their indoctrinating slimming propaganda all year round, but they become even more vociferous as summer approaches. Articles and advertisements tell us how important it is to be slim and they compete to produce one effective diet after another. 'Summer will soon be here and your figure will be on view. Is it up to it?', wrote a women's magazine in 1944.[11] 'SUMMER SLIM NOW! SUMMER SLIM – LOSE 5 KILOS IN ONE WEEK' were the headlines on the front page of a women's magazine in 1989. And so that readers should be in no doubt about the gravity of the matter, there was a picture of a tape measure across the front of the magazine and a free calorie counter inside.[12]

The message is the same year after year: you have to be slim if you want to look presentable in the smart summer and bathing clothes featured in all the magazines. However, it is not just the shape of a woman's body that is criticized if it becomes a little too rounded; its owner is accused, too, of a lack of self-discipline, and it is this aspect of the cult of slimness particularly that has led to contempt for fat people. 'What about your figure? Is it slim or do its curves and bulges reveal that you don't have enough willpower with regard to sweet and fatty foods?'[13] The copy is from an advertisement for slimming tablets in the July 1944 edition of a women's magazine, but it is not significantly different from more recent advertisements for slimming programmes, nearly all of which aim to make women feel guilty about being overweight.

In our modern consumer society a slim, well-trained body is beautiful and the object of admiration, but it is also a sign of self-control. And the fact that slimness has been emphasized as a personal value has contributed to the increasing incidence of anorexia nervosa. Sufferers believe that their starvation diet gives them control over their own bodies and, through this, the autonomy they feel they have been lacking. At the same time they live up to the demands of society and fashion for slimness.[14]

Many authors who write about anorexia maintain from studies that eating disorders occur mainly in girls who have grown up in competitive families, often with a dominating mother whose relationship with the daughter is characterized by unreasonable control and exaggerated expectations that the daughter be clever and successful.[15] When a girl becomes anorexic and starves herself it is often the result of a number of more complicated conflicts in her relationship with her parents rather than a simple desire to be slim. Nonetheless, these girls are influenced by the way society constantly stresses slimness as a route to value and status, and they do not recognize their starvation diet as abnormal or destructive until it has gone too far.

The emaciated body of an anorexic is the most extreme form of the cult of slimness, but a lot of women regard the shape of their bodies and their weight as a problem they have constantly to struggle with, often at the expense of their health. This is even more absurd when one takes into account that the cult of health is even more widespread today then ever before. One may be led to suspect that the emphasis on health has more to do with commercial interests; if a healthy exterior were no longer part of the ideal body, perhaps it would not be so important.

The fashion and beauty industries can always sell their products by fabricating new ideal images which also appeal to more liberated women, who rarely like to admit that it is important to them to be attractive. Various methods are used to keep such women locked into the despotic game of fashion and beauty. Barbara Sichtermann writes:

I believe that the challenge for women to 'look after' themselves and the fiction that the privilege of looking good can be made popular is a product of this century's wave of democratisation and principally of this wave's cultural and consumption offshoots as they have been promoted via the media and mass consumption. Democracy is not only political, it is also material. And it is an in-built demand of this material democracy to make luxury into mass consumption, i.e. to make it available to all.[16]

She believes that women are given a promise that beauty can be bought and is therefore attainable by the majority. But in reality it is a limited resource:

Beauty is as rare as a black swan. If beauty were as commonplace as having two hands and two feet, one would no longer notice it and all the longings, fictions and lies which are attached to its actual or supposed attainability would be superfluous. Beauty opposes democratisation.[17]

She is quite right. It is desirable to be slim because it is difficult and often demands time and money. If everyone had the same opportunity to stay slim, the ideal of slimness would quickly be replaced by another status ideal.

The tightly laced corset was dangerous. It deformed the ribcage and damaged the internal organs, but it was worn anyway because it was a status symbol. The modern cult of suntanned slimness also presents health risks, but that does not stop people experimenting with new health and slimming systems or lying too long in the sun.

Even if class differences have been reduced, there are still external signs and distinctions of status. The growth of the modern consumer society in which there are no in-built class barriers, other than those set by people's finances, has assisted in this breakdown of social class divisions. This has resulted in the pursuit of individuality, which is where the body and its coverings naturally play a central role. But it is an illusion to believe that we can escape entirely from the social and aesthetic demands the mass media and the beauty and fashion industries constantly force upon us. The body remains to some extent a bearer of status and social control. Even if we distance ourselves from fashion and the demand to be attractive, we continue to be a part of the social system and its organization, and new signs of status, style and taste will replace the old and make their mark on our bodies – and on how we present them.

Elegant evening gowns with tight-fitting bodice going right down over the hips, 1877.

2 Morality, Perception of the Body and Aesthetics

Baudelaire wrote that what struck him as important about old fashion plates was that they all reflected the morality and aesthetic values of their day. The body, the face, the costume – everything reflects the spirit of the time. In any form of art, including that of clothing the human form, we enjoy appreciating the complex network of currents that flow through a period, of which normally only one becomes dominant.[1] The changing ideal of beauty is an expression of a specific epoch, its style, taste, morality and attitudes.

Some costume historians have attempted to demonstrate the close connection between tightly laced corsets and moral attitudes by pointing out that periods without corsets have been characterized by loosely hanging clothes and a looser morality – for example, the period between the French Revolution and the 1820s – whereas from around 1830 to 1890 women's bodies were characteristically covered under layers of clothing and the corset was laced tightly: at the same time, self-control and a strict sexual morality were the order of the day. They have mentioned two periods where this particular analysis holds, but there are other factors that should be highlighted because it is not always the case that tight corsets are indicative of strict morality.

Apart from the period from the 1790s until the 1820s, when dresses were worn without a corset for a foundation, upper-class women wore a tight-fitting laced corset throughout most of the eighteenth and nineteenth centuries. But the shape of the female ideal was different in the eighteenth and nineteenth centuries and the ideal varied from one culture to another. Both the aristocracy and the bourgeoisie tried as dominant classes to distance themselves socially from the other classes, but their ways of living and expressing themselves were essentially different. An economic–ideological perspective clearly reveals contrasting perceptions of the body.

From around 1660 the sumptuous court of Louis XIV, the Sun King, in Versailles became the centre of fashion: from here all new fashions spread out across Europe. Europe was culturally and stylistically influenced by

Rococo lady in *grande toilette*, 1777. Elegance and gallantry were aspired to by the aristocracy in the eighteenth century.

French taste until the end of the eighteenth century. Eighteenth-century Rococo was a distinct courtly style – refined and elegant, but with a propensity for overblown luxury and elaborateness. The pleasure-seeking ideology of the aristocracy did not extend to imposing their attitudes and morality on the lower classes; on the contrary, they tried in all ways, including their adherence to this style, to distance themselves from the proletariat. Conspicuous consumption and leisure were obvious signs of rank with which the upper classes demonstrated an unproductive, useless and expensive way of life.

The body as a working tool stands in contrast to the body as a means of expression. The latter is not just a personal matter but also carries meanings that are consistent with and reinforce the ideals of the dominant class. Care of the body and its aesthetic appearance are systematized according to quite deliberate class susceptibilities.

The heavily corseted body was not an expression of a strict morality in the eighteenth century: it was a social symbol that marked class difference, an aesthetic ideal and a means of elaborate self-expression. Sexuality and eroticism were equally part of this behaviour. Seduction was actually a major art in aristocratic circles, as is excellently depicted in Pierre Choderlos de Laclos's epistolary novel *Les Liaisons Dangereuses*.

Glenn Close in elegant Rococo gown. Still from Stephen Frear's film *Dangerous Liaisons*, 1989.

The book raised an outcry when it was first published because of its portrayal of the corrupt morality of the time, its intrigues and the lives of noble idlers and libertines living on their fortunes and unearned income. It was an attack on a social class whose frivolous elegance and insatiable appetite for sensual enjoyment and luxury had got out of control. The novel's leading female character, the Marquise de Merteuil, is depicted as a dangerous, irresponsible and totally amoral woman who, with her lover, the Vicomte de Valmont, makes it a point of honour to betray both friends and enemies and with malicious enjoyment to bring about the fall of innocence wherever she can. The Marquise is a product of her era. At the same time, she is too intelligent and ambitious simply to let herself be ruled by the social conventions that compel women to be passive. So she is angry and takes revenge on behalf of her sex. In one of her letters to Valmont she writes:

Believe me, Vicomte, unnecessary virtues are rarely acquired. Since you risk nothing in your battles, you take no precautions. For you men, defeat means only one victory the less. In this unequal contest we are lucky not to lose, you unlucky when you do not win . . .

After all, to talk the jargon of love, promises reciprocally given and received can be made and broken at will by you alone: we are lucky if upon an impulse you prefer secrecy to scandal, if, content with a humiliating submission, you stop short of making yesterday's idol the victim of tomorrow's sacrifice . . .

Since, then, you have seen me controlling events and opinions; turning the formidable male into the plaything of my whims and fancies; depriving some of the will, others of the power to hurt me; since I have been capable, according to the impulse of the moment, of attaching to or banishing from my train

These tyrants that I have unseated and enslaved;

since amid a great many vicissitudes, I have kept my reputation untarnished; should you not therefore have concluded that I, who was born to revenge my sex and master yours, have been able to discover methods of doing so unknown even to myself?[2]

By taking on the role of seductress and conquering men for the sheer pleasure of it without becoming emotionally involved, she had learnt to be in control of the situation. 'Conquer or perish,' writes Madame de Merteuil at the end of the letter.[3]

Laclos, Casanova[4] and other eighteenth-century writers give us an excellent impression of life among the nobility, the leaders of fashion and cultural élite; and especially of the way in which this social class, with its taste for anything that could bring exquisite enjoyment, passed the time in the salons of Paris or held fantastic parties on their estates.

Another valuable source of learning about the shape of the eighteenth-century female ideal are the paintings and etchings of the time. These clearly reflect the prevailing morality, perception of the body and aesthetics. The French painter Antoine Watteau's poetic pictures of '*la vie galante*' beautifully depict the refined taste and dress of the upper classes in the transitional period from 1715 until about 1730, between the Baroque and Rococo. Watteau created a new genre in painting called the *fête galante*. Almost all of his paintings show the privileged classes amusing themselves with cultured courting and elegant musical gatherings against beautiful parklike backgrounds. His women are especially fascinating: they radiate exquisite grace and beauty.

In around 1715, the tall, slim figure went out of fashion and dress began to become wider. The pompous, rather stiff form of dress and court etiquette that had predominated in the last part of Louis XIV's reign was replaced by a lighter, more graceful form of dress and by more relaxed everyday social conventions.

Négligé was the term used for many of the everyday dresses that were worn on unofficial occasions. This style of dress was cut in one piece, often with deep, full-length gussets at the back. These characteristic folds were later called Watteau pleats, because Watteau often painted his female subjects in these graceful garments. Although the material hung loosely, a hoop skirt and stays were often worn underneath. The wide, richly folded dresses made women look cone-shaped.

At the beginning of the 1700s, when fashion dictated wider skirts, a tight waist and a deep neckline, the hoop skirt was resurrected as the second type of crinoline in dress history. The stiffened stays and hoop skirt of rough canvas with hoops of whalebone sewn in formed the basis for the shape of the dress.

The corset, or stays (as the corset was then called), was strongly stif-

The Two Cousins by Antoine Watteau, *c.* 1719. The loose négligé dress has so-called Watteau pleats at the back.

Mid-eighteenth-century corset made of coarse linen with splayed basque and pocket panniers with wooden hoops, worn over a fine white linen shift.

fened with strips of whalebone, set close together. It had a deep neckline, shoulder straps and splayed basque and it was normally made of rough canvas without any form of decoration. The stays of the Rococo period were funnel-shaped and went down into a point at the front. French stays were usually tied at the back, English stays at the front. It was fashionable to have a high bust, so a flat piece of wood was inserted at the front which was lifted at the same time as the laces were tightened and in this way the bust was pulled up. Before a lady put on a ball gown, her waist would be reduced little by little by tightening the laces until it reached the desired dimensions.

A half-length shift of white linen with a wide neck and sleeves was worn under the stays. Knickers for women were, however, hardly ever mentioned in literary sources. A narrow waist was essential, so laced corsets were used from a very early age. When babies were past their tenderest age, both sexes were put into a frock stiffened at the waist. From the age of four or five, children were dressed as small adults. A girl wore a tight corset and hoop skirt under her dress; it was thought that the corset would both help to give the child an upright posture and the desired tiny waist. As she grew, her ribcage and waist were gradually restricted by the lacing and her body grew used to the support the corset gave. As a result, many people thought that the back muscles were weak and that it was impossible to manage without the support.[5]

In the Rococo period the French upper classes threw themselves with abandon into an existence thoroughly devoted to the pursuit of pleasure and luxury. There was total liberation from any kind of moral inhibition with regard to sex or attitudes to the body, as can be seen from the contemporary feminine ideal. Whereas Watteau's pictures of the women of the Rococo period radiate grace and flirtatiousness, the leading French painter François Boucher created a series of pictures of Rococo women full of desire and eroticism – more aware of their body and more seductive in their behaviour than ever before. The same frivolous elegance characterizes the first French fashion magazine, *La Galerie des Modes*, published between 1778 and 1787.

The upper classes' excesses and interest in elaborate display were most clearly expressed in the dress fashions of the time and these developed in bizarre and wildly extravagant directions. The bell-shaped hoop skirt was in use until around 1745, when it became flatter at the back and front and wider at the sides. The very wide skirt, in French called *pannier à coudes*, was worn on formal occasions only; pocket panniers, a smaller variant, were worn for everyday wear. These consisted of two drum-shaped hip cushions tied at the waist and hips. The pockets had hoops of whalebone or wood with fabric stretched tightly over them and with pockets inside – hence the name. Skirts reached such dimensions that a law was passed forbidding them to be wider than the width of a carriage. Women had to go through doors sideways. It required practice to look graceful in these wide

The Graham Children by William Hogarth, 1742. The two girls are wearing stiffened, laced bodices and underskirts.

La Toilette by François Boucher, 1742. The woman on the left is tying her garter.

skirts, which had the unfortunate tendency to swing upwards at the slightest breeze – presumably to the great amusement of the men.

The extreme forms that appeared in the fashions of the late Rococo period (enormous skirts and metre-high hairstyles) were a sign of the beginning of the end for a whole social class whose position of power was under threat. In France, the Revolution deprived the aristocracy of its estates; in other countries it happened in a less dramatic way.

As the privileges of rank and absolute monarchy were whittled away, the last obstacles against the rise of the expanding bourgeoisie were removed. The wealthy middle classes of the 1800s became the ruling class, their attitudes and morality prevailed, and it was they who set the fashions.

The ideology of the middle classes was liberalism, based on the concepts of freedom and progress, rooted respectively in the ideals of freedom of the French Revolution and in the material basis for development created by the Industrial Revolution. It was the changed means of production and the new economic conditions that permitted the development of a specifically utilitarian middle-class ideology built on quite different precepts from those of the pleasure-seeking aristocracy. Middle-class ideology was based on economics, but was evident at all levels, not least those associated with attitudes to the body, which was subject to absolute control. The body

'La Grande Toilette', etching of 1778. The gown is an open outer dress over an underskirt, also called a *mantua*. The elegant fashions of the Rococo ended by being over-decorated and grotesque.

became a matter for society; it had to be systematized according to what was most expedient. How could the body be disciplined so as to become an efficient tool?

The Industrial Revolution ensured that workers' bodies became of more than physical importance and were subject to greater control. When machines took over a large portion of the work, the human workforce had to be adjusted accordingly: work became more intensive, more disciplined and time-orientated. Time became a valuable and significant factor in the conditions of production. It became 'expensive'. A well-qualified and efficient workforce was needed to work in the time that the employer paid for. But, as the working classes had not been brought up to have the requisite self-control and discipline, their attitudes and morality had to be changed; they had to be taught a more ascetic and dedicated way of life so that they could become good workers.[6]

I focus on this problem because it shows clearly the strategies used by the dominant middle class to maintain power, based on principles of a rational economy and the rationalization of work, way of life and physique of the population as a condition for the growth of capitalism. This domination penetrates all areas and levels of society, so that the ideology of the ascendant class becomes the 'dominant' ideology and, as Roland Barthes points out, is presented as 'accepted' and 'natural' for society as a whole.[7] The ascetic ethic of the middle classes became 'universal' and their morality prevailed, finding expression in the system of aesthetics.

In this moral rearmament middle-class women embodied puritanical middle-class ideology; they became its ideal. But there was a price to pay.

The corseted female body of the 1800s was the image both of middle-class self-discipline and of a restrictive sexual morality, which literally locked women into a role in which it was almost a duty to be attractive. Their beauty and dress made them into 'valuable' and visible signs of their husbands' wealth. At the same time, a puritanical moral sensibility denied women any form of physical enjoyment: they had to suppress their own desires and passions and limit the purpose of their bodies to producing legitimate children. It was only their outward appearance that compensated middle-class women for their privations, giving them a substitute for fulfilment, which resulted in physical ambiguities that can be difficult to interpret and are accordingly interpreted in various ways.

The British author David Kunzle maintains that the corset cannot simply be seen as a symbol of the oppression of women, but as having an ambivalent meaning: at once oppression and self-expression.[8] Kunzle points out that the abolition of the corset is normally connected with women's liberation, but that new expressions of 'femininity' with oppressive aspects have emerged instead. This is most clearly seen in our current extreme breast fixation: various types of bra have lifted, pointed and formed women's breasts to the ideal size and shape – a function that corresponds to that of the corset in the past, says Kunzle. True, the corset has not been the only oppressive item of women's clothing. But in its various forms the corset has over the past four hundred years altered the female body according to the prevalent ideals of beauty. By focusing on the erotic–fetishist aspects of this garment, Kunzle perhaps neglects the full scope of its damaging effects on women's bodies. His analysis is marred by a masculine fascination with this piece of restrictive underwear which has enclosed and bound women's bodies and thus made them into attractive and erotic objects – for men.

Kunzle wonders why women have voluntarily inflicted on themselves the kind of pain that this constriction of the body causes. 'Are women masochists?' he asks. The answer is that of course women do not have a particular predisposition to masochism, nor do they welcome the pain of being trussed up in a corset; this is one of the many myths about 'the nature of women'. But they have been obliged to conform to the moral and aesthetic norms of the day.

It was certainly partly of their own volition that women wore tight-fitting corsets, and yet it cannot be called a free choice. There were very few alternatives to marriage for women. The upbringing and education of girls was geared towards marriage and child-bearing. And if they wanted to be noticed on the marriage market, they had to be attractive; that is, to live up to the current ideal of beauty. The corset shaped the body so that it met this requirement and women had to submit to the social pressure to wear it.

Advertisement for Duzaine Hansen's corsets, 1896.

Advertisement for the 'bandalette' corset, 1902.

As the middle classes became predominant, the position of women deteriorated. Technical development – and the consequent social changes – brought a differentiation of men's and women's social roles and areas of work. Women were reduced to being decorative objects and moral guardians, in sharp contrast with men, who led a free and active life. Women of the middle classes became respectable, virtuous models of the ideals that were the cornerstones of the middle-class way of life. Middle-class sexual morality, which stressed restraint and self-discipline, was more strictly enforced for women than for men – 'respectable' men often operated double standards where their sex lives were concerned. The daughters of the middle and upper classes were sacrosanct and were expected to be virgins when they married; but it was not unusual for the master of the house to molest the servant girl, who was not of such high rank.

Much of the criticism that has been levelled at the moral sense of men at the end of the nineteenth century is justified: many middle-class men were hypocrites who did not themselves live up to the moral standards they set for the rest of society.

Ethics and morality were universal terms for the ancient Greeks, but differed in practice for free men, women and slaves. Michel Foucault quotes an apologia which is attributed to the Greek orator and statesman Demosthenes (383–322 BC), in which part of his argument runs as follows: 'We have courtesans for pleasure; concubines for day-to-day occupations; wives to have legitimate offspring and to be loyal guardians of the home.'[9]

As in Classical times, most patriarchal societies have distinguished between the moral practice that is prescribed for men and for women. The

The Morning Stroll by Thomas Gainsborough, 1875, showing fashionable British dress in a lighter, simpler style.

ideals of freedom and equality of the liberal period created some hope for greater equality between the sexes; but in fact the freedom was relative – it did not include women and most definitely not their bodies, the appearance and presentation of which were subject to strict control. The ideals behind the French Revolution liberated women's bodies; the restrictive morality and puritanical attitudes of the middle classes, generally speaking, reined them in again.

There was a difference, however, between the form of the ideal image in, for example, Britain and France, reflecting differing attitudes to morality and the body. The light, loose chemise dresses of the Directoire and Empire periods were worn without corsets and were more daring in France than in Britain, and the new crinolines with their tightly laced corsets and numerous underskirts were more virtuous and modest in Georgian Britain.

The fashions of the Rococo never developed to extremes in Britain. The dress of the upper classes was fashionable, but less ornamented than in France. As early as the mid-eighteenth century the relatively simple and comfortable dress of the landed gentry began to gain ground all over Britain. Dress became more democratic. This was mainly the result of the more liberal and progressive thinking prevalent in the upper and middle classes, which created good conditions for the growth and development of industrial capital. The growing British textile industry concentrated on materials such as cotton – in contrast to the silk industry in France. And, influenced by the British gentry's simple clothes, white cotton dresses for women and plain clothes for men became very fashionable in the 1780s and quickly spread to other countries.

In France, too, there were significant changes in thinking among the cultural élite from around the middle of the century. But here the ideas were mostly applied in the intellectual sphere: there was less eagerness for reform. One of the most important and pioneering philosophers of the Enlightenment was Jean-Jacques Rousseau, who tried through his writings to promote ideas about freedom, equality and democracy. His liberal thoughts and his vision of a rigorously democratic society paved the way for the bourgeois French Revolution. But even though these ideas were discussed in the noble salons of Paris and became popular in educated circles, the nobility had no thought of giving up their privileges and wealth; it was only in their clothing that they were influenced by his natural philosophy and enthusiasm for Classical times. Rousseau believed that society's only salvation was to return to nature, preferably by adopting the 'natural' form of dress and way of life prevalent in Greek and Roman times.

The writings of art historian J. J. Winckelmann and his excavations of Pompeii and Herculaneum, which had begun in the 1740s, contributed to a renewed interest in Classical times and art, which developed into a new style called neo-Classicism. The Classical tendency that characterized the dress of the 1780s was the forerunner of the dress of the Revolution and the Empire. The Classical ideal corresponded to the Revolution's demand for freedom and equality. The elegant but overdecorated court style of the Rococo gave way to a simple, relatively loose-hanging dress which fell in soft folds around the figure. The loose chemise dress, made of thin white silk or cotton, was a new fashion creation. The chemise was a whole dress cut in one piece, held together by a sash at the waist and ribbons on the sleeves. It was worn with a less stiffened and more loosely laced corset and when it first appeared it aroused great indignation.

Reforms had thus already occurred in clothing before the Revolution – the dictatorship of French fashion had been partly broken. French fashion still dominated on formal occasions, but British fashion won through for everyday dress.[10]

High-waisted fashion appeared at the beginning of the 1790s and lasted until the end of the 1820s. The chemise dress of fine, white muslin or batiste fell softly around the figure from a high waist. A corset was not

normally worn under the high-waisted dress and a minimum of under-wear was worn: a thin skirt or tight trousers made of silk jersey were often the only undergarments. The abolition of the corset undoubtedly gave women a sense of freedom.

The loosely hanging chemise dress of the Directoire and Empire peri-ods developed in France into an almost 'naked' fashion. The French taste for sophistication and sauciness is always reflected in women's clothing: in this period the dress became provocatively see-through and had such a deep neckline that nothing was left to the imagination. This fashion de-manded a good figure and an absence of blemishes. The corset had become unfashionable and instead women resorted for help to various types of short corset and bra-like sashes whose function was to push up the bust.

The dress of the late Empire was still high-waisted, but by the end of the 1820s the waistline had gradually dropped until it resumed its natural po-sition and the slim waist could again be accentuated. The corset was

Madame Récamier,
French ideal of
Empire beauty, in thin
chemise with deep
neckline, by François
Gérard, 1802.

reintroduced, but now it was a garment that went further down over the hips. Skirts became wider and an increasing number of underskirts were worn. The corset and underskirts formed the basis for a new fashionable shape – the 'hourglass' figure – a broad upper body, wasp waist and wide skirt. In the 1830s so-called 'leg-of-mutton' sleeves appeared: these were wide across the shoulders. The tight constriction of the waist was accentuated by the enormous width of the sleeves and skirts.

The middle-class woman of the Romantic period was expected to be shy and sensitive and she fainted often at the slightest provocation – the corset probably played a part in this! As the middle classes took up their place as the fashion-setting social group, the feminine ideal was transformed into an aesthetic expression of their attitudes and morality. The middle-class woman's role was based around the home. The tightly laced corset and the numerous underskirts underlined the woman's restricted social position. Queen Victoria, with her strict morality and conservative attitude to life, became a model for the British middle classes. She left her mark on the style, taste, attitudes and morality of an entire era – hence the term 'Victorian' for all the aspects of the society she influenced during her reign.

The crinoline of the new Rococo period, the third type of crinoline in history, got its name from the French word for horsehair – *crin* – the hems of the many skirts being stuffed with horsehair to give volume. Gradually, the weight of the skirts became unbearable and around 1856 they were replaced by a dome-shaped steel frame consisting of steel hoops hung on straps; it was lighter and gave greater freedom of movement than the numerous underskirts. The crinoline frame had the disadvantage of flying up in windy weather and so it became necessary to wear long knickers to maintain decency.

Trousers had until now been a masculine item of clothing, only sporadically worn by women and mostly used in non-European female dress. Female dancers and actors were required to wear knickers when they performed, but for respectable women they were regarded as almost indecent. From around 1815 small girls began to wear long knickers, which were visible under the dress – so-called pantalettes, which consisted of two long, loose trouser legs, held up at the waist with tapes and edged with lace or embroidery at the bottom.

The tight, flesh-coloured jersey trousers worn by fashionable women in the Directoire period and at the beginning of the Empire were not really knickers; rather, they were used to give the impression that the wearer was naked when she was not[11] and to protect against the cold in the winter.

Some of the earliest known knickers for women date from the beginning of the nineteenth century and come from Britain. They are wide, open garments of cotton or silk, made in two separate pieces held together at the waist and tied just under the knee with tapes. They were originally used mostly by upper-class women for riding or other sports, and were later adopted more widely. Even though women had not previously worn knickers, their numerous underskirts protected them from the cold. But with the appearance of the light and airy crinoline it now became unseemly not to wear an undergarment. The open form of knickers continued until around the turn of the century, but the lower edging gradually became more decorative, with lace and other trimmings similar to those found on other underwear.

The larger crinoline dresses were most suitable for court wear and the Empress Eugénie became their most famous exponent. Eugénie married Napoleon III in 1853 and for a time the court in Paris became the centre of fashion again – a new Rococo period in which the beautiful Eugénie was the queen of fashion in elegant creations by Worth, the leading fashion designer of the day. Enormous quantities of material and steel went into

Corset with long, firm busk in front and inset gussets, 1830.

Fashionable walking dress, 1835.

crinolines. Women from all levels of society wore crinoline dresses – a practice made possible because the crinoline frame had become mass-produced – but the size and execution of the dresses reflected clear differences in social status and the upper classes displayed the most conspicuous wastefulness to distance themselves from the lower classes.

Queen Victoria in Britain and Empress Eugénie in France both influenced the shape of the feminine ideal, each in her own way. Crinolines became widespread in these two countries and in others and, in a way that is characteristic of the period, the great contrasts between these two women were united in this fashion. The crinoline seemed, because of its size, to be an impregnable fortress, designed to keep the opposite sex at bay; but at the same time it was a seductive form of dress which, by completely concealing the lower half of a woman, intensified the curiosity about this part of her body.

Contrast was characteristic of the fashionable female body and dress in the second half of the nineteenth century – at once seductive and very respectable. Until around 1880, the seductive aspect lay in the constriction of the waist and the partial concealment of the attractions of the female body. Subsequently the fashionable body was made increasingly erotic: female contours were more strongly accentuated in a style of dress that hugged the corseted form more closely.

Young woman in crinoline frame, 1856. The light and airy crinoline fashion made the use of drawers essential for women.

Full-sized crinoline fashion, 1861. The voluminous skirts carried on crinoline frames accentuated the small corseted waist.

The corset transformed the female body into an erotic and aesthetic object, adapted to men's dream images of women. It had a clearly erotic function: close to the body and tightly laced, it conjured up associations with eroticism and control. Kunzle believes that the corset's tight lacing and, particularly, the acts of lacing and unlacing, associated with 'binding' and 'loosing', had symbolic sexual power, more than did the feminine form produced by the corset.[12]

The heavy corset ceased to be the foundation for the shape of varying fashions at the beginning of the twentieth century, but it has lived on as an erotic fetish object. This is most visible in films in which, since the 1930s, actresses have appeared in exciting and sophisticated corsets designed to make the female body into an erotic object and probably raise the pulse of the male members of the audience. This lasted until the 1970s, when feminists condemned any kind of erotically attractive and seductive clothing as a symbol of the oppression of women. Nowadays silk and lace underwear are especially associated with eroticism, but the tightly laced corset and other forms of lacing, often in black leather, are also still used in more intimate circumstances for their potential to excite and stimulate. These forms of lacing, both erotic and painful, are called 'bondage', and they often form part of the sexual repertoire of sado-masochists in particular.

Lacing the Corset by Numa Bassaget, 1830.

Brigitte Bardot and Jeanne Moreau in the seductive clothing of 1900. Still from the film *Viva Maria*, 1965.

Playing with bondage does not signal submission: black satin laced top by Yves Saint-Laurent and black shorts by Katharine Hamnett, *Vogue*, 1991.

The varying aesthetic forms of the female body contain a complexity of meanings; the corset in particular is the bearer of many contradictory symbolic meanings which are impossible to understand unless they are seen in connection with the morality and attitudes prevalent at the time. Any change of attitude in society and between the sexes has an immediate and obvious influence on the shape of new developments in fashion.

Hunting party at the court of Duke Philip of Burgundy, c. 1450. This painting shows the growing accentuation of the female forms in the fashion of the day.

3 Dress and Fashion

Dress and fashion are not identical terms, although they both clothe the body. What makes clothes into objects of fashion?

In his book *On Liberty* (1859) John Stuart Mill wrote that the fundamental characteristic of fashion is its changeability and thus its ability to create renewal in clothing. This has not, however, led to a higher degree of individuality: people still all try to wear the same clothes, because fashionable clothes, like other forms of dress, are subject to social control.

We have discarded the fixed costumes of our forefathers: everyone must still dress like other people, but the fashion may change once or twice a year. We thus take care that when there is a change, it shall be for change's sake and not from any idea of beauty or convenience; for the same idea of beauty and convenience would not strike all the world at the same moment; and be simultaneously thrown aside by all at the same time.[1]

The very nature of fashion is contradictory. It dictates what the ideal body and dress must look like at any given time and subjugates all clothes to its demands, thus tending to make everyone's clothes look similar; at the same time, the frequent changes in fashion form a barrier to prevent everyone from following the fashion. It is not one of the tenets of fashion that everyone should dress identically. Fashion has a clear function of distinguishing between ranks and classes. But since dress is well suited to the acquisition of prestige, most people try to adopt the form of dress that carries the highest status; as it becomes more and more popular, it gradually loses its effect as a status symbol and so new fashion signals have to be produced.

The principle of fashionable dress is that it should be international, that it should change quickly, promote innovation and imitation – and be created for the élite. There is a contrast here both with earlier 'high cultural' dress, which naturally marked social differences but remained almost unchanged for long periods, and with regional dress, which was relatively stable and was dictated collectively, in that in times of prosperity, certain aspects of fashionable dress were assimilated but adapted to common needs.

Isabella of Bavaria's entrance into Paris, 1389. The women are dressed in Burgundian fashion with high hennins, high belts and full skirts.

Fashion is principally an urban upper- and middle-class phenomenon whose development is connected with the increasing trade, capitalism and urban culture that characterized western European culture from around 1350. The economic growth of commercial towns created the right conditions for the appearance of the middle class, or third estate, and with it a more differentiated society in which dress, as a part of the whole, was an appropriate status symbol. The expanding middle class could afford to dress elegantly and fashionably but, in the view of the aristocracy, did not have the right to do so. There were attempts from governments to regulate the way the various ranks dressed by the issuing of rank and luxury ordinances. One had to be able to tell a merchant from a courtier and was not permitted to dress above one's station. Ordinances were issued to limit the consumption of luxury items. First and foremost, however, the ordinances from the king and the aristocracy were an attempt to maintain differences in rank and their own privileges. Dress was, however, so useful as a route to prestige that the ordinances were not observed.[2]

In western Europe men's and women's dress became more sex-specific from around the mid-1300s and female forms became more accentuated. Until this time both men and women had worn long, loose hanging tunics which covered the entire body. Dress for both sexes consisted of an outer tunic and an inner tunic. It is not always easy to distinguish between the outer and inner clothing of earlier times. The beginnings of underclothes – the man's shirt and the woman's shift – have their roots in the tunic and were initially used as outer clothing. It gradually became common for the

Miniature, *c.* 1330, showing the loose tunics worn by both sexes.

upper classes to wear thin garments under their outer clothing, while shirts and shifts first became common in the lower classes in the eighteenth century and served for some time as both underclothes and nightclothes.

From the mid-1300s women wore a tight-fitting bodice and the waist was accentuated. The dress was tailored and gussets inserted. Buttons were also used to enable the tight dress to be put on and taken off. A stiff linen under-bodice was worn under this new type of dress; it was called a *cotte*,[3] an early French term for what later became known as the corset. This marked the introduction of a new type of underwear which, in contrast to the shift, was intended to shape the body to the current fashion ideal. This was the start of fashionable dress, the basis of which increasingly was the corseted and moulded body.

Burgundian dress is an early example of fashionable dress. At its height, the Duchy of Burgundy was a leading power in Europe and while it retained this position – until 1477, when it was absorbed into France – the wealthy Burgundian court became the centre of fashion.[4] Fashionable dress for women consisted of a tight bodice with a deep neckline and it often had a high belt from which the wide skirt fell in soft folds. The most characteristic aspect of this dress was the tall pointed headdress called a *hennin*.

The female figure of the late Middle Ages was S-shaped – but unlike the S-shape that became the fashion ideal around 1900 and was 'stomachless', the fifteenth-century female ideal had a protruding stomach. How much this had to do with frequent pregnancy is questionable – fashion has never really made allowance for this period in a woman's life. In cultured circles women withdrew from society when pregnancy became visible. The corset could not be worn then and this was therefore the only time when the female body was released from its tight constriction.

The lightly flowing, richly folded dress of the Middle Ages appears to have controlled the body less than did the stiff and tight dress that dominated Spanish Renaissance fashion. But that folded dress, which almost concealed the body, was by no means an expression of physical liberation. The body image of the Middle Ages was restrictive and connected with the ambivalent attitude to women developed by theologians and churchmen. Their attitude towards women was a combination of adoration of the Virgin, arising out of the cult of the Virgin Mary, and a misogynistic attitude, born of sexual fear. Woman was the temptress, the Devil's tool, who prevented men achieving the salvation of their soul. In Umberto Eco's novel *The Name of the Rose*, the older monk, William, says to the younger monk, Adso, who has 'sinned':

In your defence there is the fact that you found yourself in one of those situations in which even a father in the desert would have damned himself. And of women as a source of temptation the Scriptures have already said enough. Ecclesiastes says of woman that her conversation is like burning fire, and the Proverbs say that she takes possession of man's precious soul and that the strongest men are ruined by her.[5]

The physical and sensual were toned down in the depiction of female beauty, and spiritual values accentuated. But towards the end of the Middle Ages there was a change in attitude, mainly owing to the growth of trade and economic development and burgeoning humanism – a new secular and aesthetic intellectual movement that became the basis for Europe's intellectual and artistic life over the following centuries.[6] Thus the power of the Church was weakened. It had always been one of the Church's great strengths that religion embraced just about every aspect of human life, both spiritual and earthly. Humanism's 'modern' view of life was free of this religious and social connection and held simply that the aim of human effort was human development in all areas.

The Renaissance represented a rebirth of the ideals of the Classical period. Gombrich has written that the Middle Ages are so called because

Venus and Cupid with an Organist by Titian, 1545–8, shows the soft rounded forms of the naked feminine ideal.

the period lay between the original Classical period and the time of the re-naissance of Classical ideals.[7] Renaissance people did not want to copy the ancients, merely to use elements from the Classical past freely in order to create new forms of harmony and beauty. They released themselves both ethically and aesthetically from the bonds of Christian attitudes to life and the body. The naked body once again became the object of unrestrained delight and interest. Michelangelo devoted himself almost exclusively to the depiction of the naked human body, most often that of the male. Bot-ticelli, Titian and Raphael, on the other hand, had a predilection for the female body and idealized its beauty, richness and grace without exagger-ated emphasis on sensuality or sexuality.

Comparison of a picture of the ideal naked female of the period with a clothed ideal shows that they send different signals. In Titian's painting *Venus and Cupid with an Organist* (c. 1550) the female form is round and full; but contemporary paintings of women dressed in the fashionable dress of the upper classes were based on quite different principles. It is not just the fabric and the accessories that indicate the woman's social status; the body itself, reshaped by a corset, also acquires meaning. The Renaissance was the time when the practice of adapting the body and its clothes to fit an aesthetic ideal came to full expression. The marked differ-ence that arose then in the way the naked and the clothed figure were depicted in art persisted until the beginning of the twentieth century, when the ideal of slimness became a dominant aesthetic in Western cul-ture. In today's most prevalent form of art, photography, only the slim body characterizes both the naked and the clothed body ideal.

In *La Belle Nani* by Paolo Caliari, *c.* 1550, the clothed feminine ideal is reliant on a corset.

Northern Italian commercial towns were the centre of international trade in the early Renaissance: they had such economic power that they also dominated the period culturally and stylistically. A state's position as an economic power brings with it dominance in nearly all areas. Changes in style, always connected with significant changes in society, follow the shift of dominance between states. The styles of a period in architecture, domestic design, art and dress evolve in parallel and express the spirit of the time, but they are also conditioned by the cultural identity of the dominant power.

Spanish Renaissance fashion with tight bodice and stiff, funnel-shaped skirt, *c.* 1547.

The Renaissance gave rise to new ways of looking at the world: the high forms of the Gothic period, reaching heavenwards, were superseded in the 1500s by wide, articulate forms, most clearly seen in the architecture and dress of the time. The slim figure and soft, richly folded dress changed form; skirts became wider and the waist tighter, and stiff, heavy and expensive fabrics were used. The extravagance and shape of the dress were an expression of the global expansion of the western European economy. The upper classes demonstrated their power and material wealth with large, luxurious dresses which were designed to be noticed, and the increasing ease of travel allowed fashion to spread more quickly. Fashionable dress became international – a common mode of expression for the upper classes – but since it quickly spread to other social classes, it had to be replaced regularly by new fashions.

Italy lost its economic power at the beginning of the sixteenth century. From around 1550 to 1600 Spain was the focus of Europe's economic and cultural life, and its style became known as the 'Spanish Renaissance'. From around 1550, female dress began to be divided into bodice and skirt, both stiffened; a new technique meant that the dress could be cut tighter in the bodice and wider in the skirt. The new stiff, tight dress was closely connected with the morality dominant in Spain. The dress was

Iron corset from the early sixteenth century.

often dark and tightly buttoned, expressing self-control. The female silhouette consisted of two conical forms, joined at the apex, and the body was adapted to fit this shape.

In order to achieve the tight and stiff shape of the dress, two new items of underwear were introduced. The corset, already in existence as a stiff inner bodice but not previously used as the actual foundation for the shape of a dress, was now designed so that, with the aid of inserted wooden, metal or whalebone stays, it pushed the bust up and flattened it, at the same time emphasizing a tightly laced waist. The corset had a long, firm busk at the front and it was this that formed the basis of the stiffening. Spanish Renaissance style introduced the first crinoline in history, called a *vertugade* or *vertugale* (guardian of virtue),[8] in English called a farthingale. This totally new piece of underwear was a wide, funnel-shaped linen or felt underskirt, which was tied at the waist. In order to give it the right weight and shape, hoops of whalebone or metal were sewn in.

Some of the earliest known corsets were made of iron. They consisted of iron plates with hinges and locks and seem to suggest the strictest physical control. There is a difference of opinion about the function of the iron corset, however: some people think it had an orthopaedic function, others that it served merely as stiffening for the dress in the same way as other corsets. Iron corsets from the sixteenth century have the same shape as other corsets and thus probably had the same function.

Spanish fashionable dress spread to the rest of Europe, with certain variations, but the tight corset and the stiffened skirt were generally the basis of an upper-class woman's dress. Without the corset she was regarded as undressed and would be scorned. The stiff Spanish farthingale persisted in Spain into the seventeenth century and grew to prodigious widths. Meanwhile, the French and British farthingale developed another form:

Queen Elizabeth I of England in drum farthingale, by Marcus Gheeraerts the Younger, *c.* 1592.

the barrel or cartwheel crinoline, held in shape by hoops sewn into the skirt, later with the addition of a round, padded cushion worn around the hips under the skirt. This cushion was known as a 'bum roll' and was sometimes used as a less extreme alternative to the stiffened skirts. The drum-shaped farthingale became fashionable in several countries. It is best known in Britain from Elizabeth I's imposing dresses, with the long, stiff bodice ending in a point, the padded sleeves and the large, starched collars.

The chemise, the corset and the underskirt had come to stay, as integral components of female dress, for the next three hundred years, with the exception of the period from immediately after the French Revolution until the 1820s, during which the chemise became an outer garment and the corset and underskirt all but disappeared. The long linen or cotton chemise kept the same loose shape during the entire period whereas the corset and underskirt changed shape according to the fashion of the time, since they provided its basic shape.

Previously the corset had often been sewn into the bodice or worn as an outer garment made of starched linen and completely concealed under a covering of expensive fabric. From the end of the seventeenth century the corset appeared mostly as a separate under-bodice. Early corsets were called a 'body' (or 'pair of bodies') in English and *corps* in French. By the eighteenth century the English name had become 'stays' and the French *corset*.[9]

Roland Barthes imposes a semiological view on the study of Classical subject areas, including the study of fashion. He believes that the sign elements do not mean anything in themselves but that they become bearers of meaning, inasmuch as they are the expression of collective values: all clothing bears a formally organized system of signs, as determined by the dominant class. There are conventions connected with dressing – meanings are attached to the individual elements and to the way the elements are combined. He points out that costume research ought not only to classify the types of dress, but also to investigate and interpret rules for the use of dress.[10]

In *Système de la mode*, Barthes analyses fashion as a literary system, that is as it manifests itself in the form of text in fashion magazines. In this way he reveals fashion as rhetorical. The text prescribes what 'the woman of fashion' should be (identity) and do (active situations). She is what the female reader is and, at the same time, what she dreams of being. The dream is an important ingredient in all the dressing-up games fashion suggests. Barthes's belief is that fashion has no content at all except on the level of rhetoric: the fashion system creates meanings by encoding signs and symbols (by projecting a specific meaning onto them). Things become signs with meanings such as *modern* and *out-of-date*.

French fashion plate, 1835, and Danish fashion plate, 1928. Two widely differing expressions of feminine beauty.

'Every woman will shorten her skirts to just above the knee.'[11] Such a message is, as Barthes points out, almost tyrannical even if its formulation is quite innocent. The message is that you will be out of date if you do not shorten your skirt. And what could be worse than that? It is a decree that has to be obeyed! To Barthes, the way in which fashion transforms a particular article into a 'fashionable' article is fatal. Fashion can force any body at all into the structure it has postulated by tricks that reduce, enlarge, lengthen, etc., so that the physical body is turned into the fashionable body.

Barthes makes a very detailed study of the linguistic meanings of the various elements of dress and how they can be varied and combined in several ways to achieve different meanings. His main intention is to construct a method which systematizes the meanings in the fashion system step by step; the system of meanings that is attached to clothes in the texts of the fashion magazines has a function of social classification. Barthes discusses the way in which elements within the fashion system temporarily become 'attractive' because they have had a meaning ascribed to them that is not identical to their actual meaning. This is an important area of study, but his method is perhaps too clinical; it is an analysis stripped of all functions of meaning other than the 'true codes' in the text's description of fashion. Without reference to the cultural context, this system sheds light on one aspect only of the complex conundrum of fashion.

There is an element of despotism in fashion's dictates. If we do not follow them, we go beyond what is acceptable. But many people follow fashion simply because they are fascinated by its exciting and challenging offers of new forms of self-expression. Fashion offers new ways of looking attractive and of showing 'who one is'. The element of coercion resides mainly in the fact that we find it hard to avoid the changing decrees of fashion; it irritates us and we may even perceive it as tyrannical. Most of us have an ambivalent attitude to fashion.

Karen Blixen loved to stage her own roles and appear in elegant and expensive fashionable clothes and full war-paint: she regarded external expression as a reflection of the inner self. In her book *Daguerreotypes*, she reflected on the various cultural phenomena which, like old photographs, reproduce not only the people of the day, dressed in their best clothes, but also their ideas, ideals and views of life. The photographs, which at the time were modern portraits of people in fashionable dress, quickly went out of date. Now they are cultural history – snapshots of a period and its ideology. Karen Blixen thought that this strange development was especially true of clothing:

I have wondered from time to time during my life about the fact that mute objects which are put aside in drawers or on shelves, and which are not attacked by moths or rust, undergo drastic changes in their existence during the course of years.

I have seen it happen in Africa with my party dresses which I bought in Europe and hung up in a closet - and when I took them out to wear after two or three years . . . they turned out to be much too long or much too short. They had not changed, but were nevertheless changed. The styles and my own eyes were responsible for the change.[12]

If new fashions are to catch on, they have to be in tune with prevailing ideals. The attitudes and morality of a society are important factors – what is 'beautiful' is conditioned by contemporary perception of the 'ideal'. Baudelaire pointed out that every age creates just that expression of beauty that is demanded; expressions which contain both 'beauty' and 'ugliness' are contradictory and ambiguous. Every age sets its 'modern mark' on human appearance.[13] Baudelaire puts his finger on some essential points, because he takes into account the irrational and ambiguous aspects of fashion, which make it impossible, for example, to explain why we wear clothes that cause us pain and why our liking for certain fashions seems incomprehensible ten years later.

Fashion alone does not create the changing 'ideals of femininity'; different aesthetic body ideals have also existed in cultures before fashion became dominant and similarly in cultures in which the fashion phenomenon barely exists, if at all. The most characteristic aspect of fashion is its ability to transform objects into symbols. Clothes are transformed into fashion garments and the body becomes the fashion body.

English fashion doll in wood, *c.* 1750.

4 Propagation of the Fashion Ideal

The growth of western European commercial towns in the late Middle Ages provided the right conditions for the growth of capitalism and the more obvious appearance of fashion, the development of which in both cases relies on economic principles. A state or urban society fluctuated between being a commercial centre or a peripheral area according to its level of commercial activity and its position as a traffic junction on the trade route (although this position was not stationary, but changed as new trade destinations developed). The flourishing commercial centres represented an accumulation of capital, which gave them a fluctuating economic supremacy; at the same time they could enjoy a position as centres of culture and style, in which the court and nobility decided which ideals and tastes would prevail.

Changing fashions within a stylistic period were partly an expression of the ideal in the prevalent taste, and partly an expression of fashion as a phenomenon of novelty and dissemination. The holders of power wished their taste to be both national and international; their dress was to be seen and admired by others and spread to other courts – but not to other social groups.

The dissemination of new fashions from the leading centre of innovation to other European courts is known from as early as the fourteenth century, when dolls dressed in the latest fashions were exchanged between the most exclusive courts. These dolls were not children's toys but were produced in the service of fashion. They may well have been given to children to play with afterwards, but this was not their primary function.

The earliest known fashion dolls date from the late fourteenth century when Isabella of Bavaria sent fully equipped dolls to the Queen of England to demonstrate the fashions at the court of Burgundy, the leading court of the day. Burgundy remained a cultural centre for most of the fifteenth century and many fashion dolls were sent from there to other European courts.

Louis XIV's extravagant court at Versailles became the ideal for other European courts from around 1660 and French fashion reigned supreme.

Distinctive carved wooden doll, *c.* 1580, possibly of French origin.

Fashion dolls were distributed and two fully dressed dolls were sent regularly from the Palais Rambouillet in rue St Honoré in Paris to the other courts. Made of painted wood and about 90 cm high, they were called 'big Pandora' and 'little Pandora', not because of their size but because of the way they were dressed – full toilet and négligé respectively.[1]

With the distribution of such dolls awareness of French fashions and textiles was spread widely and France reinforced its position as the arbiter of style. This propagation of fashion was of great importance for the country: it was not simply a demonstration of its taste but it also had a strategic purpose, in that it was intended to secure the French textile industry, which was a requirement for the development of French fashion supremacy.

This relationship can be seen clearly in the Empire period: this was a bad time for the French silk industry, when the light chemise made of white cotton was the most popular fashion item. Around 1810 Napoleon forbade the import of muslin, batiste and other fine materials, arguing, probably correctly, that fine materials were not suited to the climate in Paris. The real reason was that he was trying to resurrect the silk industry in Lyons. The soft cotton materials were replaced by thicker materials such as taffeta, satin and velvet and these produced a stiffer profile in dresses.

The distribution of fashion dolls from Paris to the other European capitals continued through the eighteenth century and culminated in the

1780s with the fashion clothes which Marie Antoinette's minister of fashion, Rose Bertin, made for the queen each week and had copied to put on dolls, often lifesize, which were sent to the queen's mother, Maria Theresa of Austria, and her sisters in Vienna. Apart from serving as messengers of new styles, these dolls also represented changing beauty and body ideals. The surviving or documented dolls all have the coveted slender waist and other characteristics that represent the then ideal of the feminine.

The French Revolution put an end to this practice; but it was no longer necessary in any case, since fashion magazines with colour plates were now being published in several countries such as Britain, France and Germany. One of the first real fashion magazines was *The Lady's Magazine* (London), published between 1770 and 1837. Only very few of the other magazines that appeared at the end of the eighteenth century survived that long. Most were relatively shortlived.[2] During the nineteenth century, a growing number of fashion magazines were published, which, with the advent of the sewing machine in 1850, made it possible for people other than the upper classes to copy and produce fashionable dress. The new fashions spread very quickly to many social groups, but the idealized body that characterized the early plates, fashion designs and later mass-produced prints was, for most people, impossible to attain. The pictorial representation of fashion idealizes the body – both men's and women's bodies are made to conform to the prevailing fashion ideal.

It is through another medium that the female body in particular has been made the object of idealization. Fine fashion dolls and mannequins reappeared in various forms in the nineteenth century and gradually became the perfect expression of the fashion and body ideal of the day. Only female dolls were produced. The term 'fashion doll' was especially used in the nineteenth century for the very beautiful and expensive French fashion dolls whose popularity was at its height from around 1860 to 1890. Their production became a major industry. One of these exclusive dolls was called *poupée parisienne* (Parisian doll), but it is uncertain whether the name referred to this specific type of doll or rather to the type of fashionable, luxurious clothes in which it was dressed.

The dolls had beautiful, pink heads made of biscuit (unglazed porcelain), with glass eyes and wigs made of animal or human hair. The bodies, which were shaped according to the current ideal of feminine beauty, were mainly made of leather, but other materials were also used. The arms or lower arms – and sometimes the legs – were made of biscuit. The dolls were between 30 and 75 cm high. Fashion dolls were used in various connections. Some were used for exhibitions in shops and fashion houses to show what the new fashions looked like on a mannequin, others were sold as toys for the children of wealthy parents. Even children's dolls

French doll with
biscuit head, dressed
in the fashion of 1870.

were dressed in the latest fashions, complete from top to toe with the appropriate clothes and accessories, and many firms published catalogues to try to encourage the owners to update the dolls' wardrobes.[3] The dolls were intended for children, but they represented fully grown women; and no doubt they helped to impress on the little girls how important it was to make oneself beautiful in order to succeed on the marriage market. The doll industry took advantage of the little girls' dreams, which were naturally oriented towards their future as adults.

The way in which the doll industry operates today is much the same as in earlier periods. The main difference is that the industry now targets all children. There is greater social equality and also much heavier advertising of these mass-produced goods. But the product itself and the little girls' dreams have changed in step with the changing feminine ideal.

In 1959 the American toy producer Mattel launched their new product, the long-legged and slender teenage doll, Barbie: 'New for '59, the Barbie doll - A shapely teenage Fashion Model!'[4] The term 'teenager' was coined in the USA after the Second World War and spread to Europe at the beginning of the 1950s. The desire of the young for an independent means of expression was quickly exploited by the commercial fashion and 'youth' industry to produce younger and different ideals in tune with the beauty

Long-legged and slender 'Barbie': the fashion doll in a modern form, 1959.

concepts of the time. The Barbie doll's slender, youthful body and well-cared-for exterior represented a new aesthetic ideal; a sophisticated dream-girl who, with her wide range of accessories, appealed to girls' fantasies that 'every girl can be a star', as the catalogue promised.

Barbie has changed her appearance in step with changing fashion ideals throughout her nearly forty-year history, so that she always reflects the prevalent ideal of young girls and women. By adapting she has thus managed to remain 'modern' and attractive. Barbie is the best-selling doll in history, because the doll and fashion industries have collaborated to produce constantly new fashion accessories to encourage variations on the Barbie theme.

The fashion dolls and mannequins of the nineteenth and twentieth centuries have not just had an effect as toys; they have in contemporary form helped to socialize children and young people to the norms and values of the adult world in which beauty and modernity rank very high. Women are not naturally 'fashion victims', even though following fashion is regarded as a female weakness, but from childhood they are constantly confronted with feminine ideals and the demand to be beautiful, pressures which are difficult to avoid.

Women became the supreme supporters and propagators of fashion in the nineteenth century, but not the only ones; from around the middle of that century women received competition from the more idealized and totally artificial mannequins then being produced. As modern urban and commercial life developed and shops increasingly used display windows to achieve more direct contact with the public, there was an increasing demand for lifesize shop-window mannequins. Previously, customers were virtually kidnapped on the street and dragged in to see the choice of goods that were available to buy; now the shops displayed their goods in the windows in order to lure customers in. Window displays were of vital importance to catch the eye and the mannequins became an important way of promoting and selling new fashions. A dress looks much better on a figure that approximates to how it would look in real life than it does on a hanger. The window-shopper should be able to identify with the model, which is provided with as many realistic characteristics as are necessary to create the impression that she could look like that, too, if she bought those clothes. But here we have an idealized version, more perfect than any human being could ever be.

Some of the earliest known display mannequins are headless dummies or dress forms made of wicker or cane. They were used in Parisian shop windows and many other places. Professor Guerre Lavigne was one of the first people to start production of mannequin busts, in about 1849. They were intended among other things for display windows in the new department stores that were opening in Paris at the beginning of the 1850s. These busts were also headless, but the bodies were shaped to conform exactly with the ideal corseted female figure, and so they were a perfect means of presenting the new fashions.

Mannequins which looked lifelike, with a head and limbs, first appeared around the 1870s; they were mainly produced in France. Fred Stockman's shop, established in Paris in 1869, was the first to display such busts and mannequins. Inspired by the French mannequins, the British company Harris and Sheldon started production of display figures in the 1880s. It became one of the largest British producers of busts, mannequin figures and other equipment for the display of goods in shops. And in 1896 Pierre Imans founded his own business and employed various artists in his workshop. He became well known for producing very fine, naturalistic wax dummies with wigs made of real hair, and with glass eyes and articulated waist and limbs.

When in 1856 Jacob Moresco opened his first milliner's shop in Copenhagen, De la Ville de Paris, he immediately thought of buying a wax dummy of the type he had seen used in shop windows in many other places in Europe. However, it was quite some time before he bought in Berlin the wax dummy on which he wanted to display his wares:

Exhibition of corsets in Duzaine Hansen's Aalborg branch, *c.* 1904.

One had to turn the dummy by hand, since there was no mechanism in it, this being too expensive for me; but I noticed that when people had stood and watched the dummy turn for a while they soon got tired of it and did not give it another glance. On the other hand, I started to dress the dummy myself each evening when the window was still illuminated and that drew attention, not just that same evening, but evening upon evening. In order to attract people's attention, I first dressed the other windows and then, when that was done, the performance began with the dummy. The street outside was immediately thick with people and, while I dressed the dummy, I could hear the coachdrivers shouting at people to get out of the way so they could pass the crowd with their horse and carriage. The number of purchases increased accordingly and I continued this profitable and very cheap advertisement every evening for many years, provided the weather was clement.[5]

Jacob Moresco exploited a new and modern display technique, then relatively unknown in Denmark, but which, with the advent of department stores from around 1850, very quickly became part of the more fashionable shop life in London and Paris. Large shops and 'bazaars' began to appear in London and several other British cities as early as the 1830s and 1840s; for example, Kendal Milne and Faulkner (originally called The Bazaar), which opened in Manchester in 1836, and Bainbridge's of Newcastle, which opened in 1838 and quickly grew into a large business with a wide

Wax mannequins dressed in the fashion of the day in the window of Magasin du Nord, Copenhagen, 1908.

range of goods. The famous Au Bon Marché in Paris, built in 1852, is generally acknowledged to have been the first department store in the world. In its architecture, displays and new business practices, it was the prototype for department stores in other European cities. The department stores operated business practices that differed from those of specialist shops. First and foremost, prices were fixed; the customer no longer bargained over the price of an article, nor was anyone coerced to buy. One could look at the window displays or walk around the various departments and buy only if one wanted to. The window mannequins quickly became popular and indispensable in the presentation of new fashions. Modern display techniques quickly became an important factor in the way department stores and specialist shops profiled themselves.

The commercialization of fashion brought with it an increasing visualization of the fashionable body – a tendency which has become even more pronounced with the development and enormous importance of fashion photography and advertising as producers and messengers of aesthetic expression in the twentieth century. Everywhere in magazines and catalogues the images signal what the fashionable body should look like.

The presentation of fashion clothes on living models or mannequins was launched as early as the nineteenth century. When the Englishman Charles Frederick Worth founded his own fashion house in Paris in 1858, the idea was not new: other creators of fashion had made clothes for the upper classes before him. But Worth's fashion house was based on principles that were different from those of earlier fashion production. The novelty was partly that Worth presented his creations on live models and partly that he chose the fabrics and produced the entire finished article himself, whereas this would previously have been done by various experts. He created a cohesive collection of fashionable clothes, designed to be copied and with an eye to selling to an exclusive clientèle. With these new ideas he became the founder of *haute couture*, which has since developed into a collection of fashion houses within a powerful union called La Chambre Syndicale de la Haute Couture Parisienne.

French *haute couture* represented attractive and well-made tailoring; it now also became a business. France has been the dominant power throughout the history of fashion – a position that it still tries to reinforce. Worth's new thinking about the dissemination of fashion marked the beginning of greater commercialization, which has accelerated through the twentieth century. The production of aesthetic articles is connected with much deeper financial interests which the whole fashion industry tries to maintain. So it is forced to renew itself constantly by producing up-to-date and attractive fashions that express social prestige and individuality.

Changeability is one of the fundamental characteristics of fashion and a condition for its existence, but this ability to transform anything into fashion symbols also means that it is almost impossible to avoid its power. Baudrillard hits the nail on the head, but is also condemnatory when he writes:

Fashion is immoral, this is what's in question . . . it knows nothing of value-systems, nor of criteria of judgement: good and evil, beauty and ugliness, the rational/irrational – it plays within and beyond these, it acts therefore as the subversion of all order, including revolutionary rationality . . . We cannot escape fashion (since fashion itself makes the refusal of fashion into a fashion feature . . .).[6]

PART II PHYSICAL ALTERATION
1880s – 1990s

5 The Corseted Woman
1880s–*c.* 1909

Throughout the period up to the turn of the century the ideal female body was moulded by a closely fitting, increasingly tightly laced corset. It was as if fashion were fighting a pitched battle against the reform efforts underway at the time to emancipate the female body from this form of armour. The corset was not a new phenomenon: it had in various incarnations formed the foundation for dresses for several hundred years. But from the late 1880s there was a radical change in both the corset and women's underwear in general; a change that must be viewed in the light of altered attitudes to the body, the appearance of new aesthetic ideals and a greater differentiation between upper- and middle-class women expressed through various physical forms.

The idealized body could be clearly seen in the physical form of artificial window dummies. During this period dummies had rounded forms and a very tightly narrowed waist, exactly matching the laced-in waist that in real women emphasized the rounding of the bust and hips. The dummies were made of wax and were produced primarily in France, where Pierre Imans was famous for his naturalism. From 1900 he presented exhibitions in his salon in Paris of wax dummies clothed in the latest fashions in dresses and corsets. Headless busts with the ideal female shape had been in use to exhibit clothes since the middle of the 1800s and from the late 1890s were used to exhibit corsets and items of lingerie.

To be able to demonstrate fashionable clothing, the dummy had to have the same form as the fashion ideal. The shape of the dummy exactly reflected the physical change that characterized the fashionable body and, at the same time, put both body and gender in the spotlight. The natural female body was concealed; instead, the remoulded and idealized body was accentuated as an erotic object. Attention was directed to a specific part of the body which, by virtue of its concealment, became titillating and the object of sexual fantasies.

Wax mannequin with corseted figure by Pierre Imans, early twentieth century.

In Karen Blixen's tale *The Old Chevalier* an old gentleman relates:

In those days a woman's body was a secret which her clothes did their utmost to keep. We would walk about in the streets in bad weather in order to catch a glimpse of an ankle, the sight of which must be as familiar to you young men of the present day as the stems of these wine-glasses of ours. Clothes then had a being, an idea of their own. With a serenity that was not easy to look through, they made it their object to transform the body which they encircled, and to create a silhouette so far from its real form as to make it a mystery which it was a divine privilege to solve. The long tight stays, the whalebones, skirts and petticoats, bustle and draperies, all that mass of material under which the women of my day were buried where they were not laced together as tightly as they could possibly stand it – all aimed at one thing: to disguise.[1]

Throughout history, the corset has been of greater importance than most other items of clothing. The necessity of corsets was consistently maintained, to such a degree that many people believed that if a dress was to fit properly, a corset was indispensable – as can be seen from an advertisement of 1900:

With regard to the great demands which are increasingly being put on the figure and, most specifically, on corsets, attention is drawn to the necessity and expedience of every lady, ladies' tailor and outfitter of acquiring a new corset fitting the figure and fashion exactly before ordering new dresses or outfits.[2]

By as early as about 1660, the cutting and fitting of corsets had become a very specialized craft, carried out exclusively by men. Many eighteenth-

Bust with corset by Duzaine Hansen, 1890s.

Advertisement for corsets, 1900.

The corsetmaker fitting a lady's corset, 1778.

century French engravings show a male tailor fitting a corset on a woman – a rather piquant scene popular among artists. As the lacing of a corset became the subject of more criticism, this situation was depicted more satirically. Seamstresses made skirts and other parts of the dress, but the garment that gave the shape was the preserve of male tailors for a long time. It was not until the 1830s that women began to establish themselves as corsetmakers. However, around the middle of the nineteenth century the entire industry met with stiff competition from the growing industrial production of corsets.

Early corsets were made of relatively few individual pieces with inserted gussets. From the 1840s, corsets were made of several shaped pieces; the short models often had no gussets, while the longer, basqued versions were gusseted. The most important part of the stiffening was the long, sturdy, wooden whalebone or steel busk at the front of the corset. From around 1840, it was replaced by a divided steel busk with a hook-and-eye system which meant that women could put on their corsets themselves, but help was still needed to lace them. Moreover, it was impossible to work wearing a corset, so women of the upper classes were still the only ones who could wear them. By the 1880s, corsets consisted of between ten and fourteen individual pieces sewn together, a long, curved busk at the front with a hook-and-eye system (often called a 'spoon busk', which was very rigid at the base), and close-set whalebone or steel stays inserted in stitched channels. Whalebone was particularly suitable for stays, because it became elastic when heated and could be moulded as required; it was used in corsets until the beginning of the 1900s.

Despite representations by doctors and reformers, corsets became even more tightly laced throughout the 1890s: a typical corseted waist measured about 47cm. In 1902 the French corset-maker Inez Gache-Sarrautes created a new corset which had a straight busk at the front. The corset created a new fashionable silhouette in which the stomach was pressed flat, the bust was pushed up and the hips were pushed back. It was called the *sans ventre* ('stomachless' or 'erect line') and it was responsible for women's curious S-shape. Naturally, it unleashed protests from many quarters, but most women ignored the attacks and it was not replaced by a less stiffened line until around 1910.

The main change in women's corsets and underwear in the late 1880s was in the use of new materials, colours and increasing decoration. Dress historian Anne Buck describes the period 1890–1914 as the great epoch of underwear.[3] During the Belle Epoque, underwear became 'lingerie' and the corset, like other underwear, became thoroughly decorative; it became fashionable to wear sophisticated clothes under one's dress. Never before had so much work been put into the actual decoration of corsets – which were not intended to be seen but whose primary function was to mould the body to the current ideal of beauty. The corset now became an attractive and aesthetic garment in its own right.

Corset with 'Spoon busk', c. 1878.

Fashion plates were produced almost exclusively in the form of drawn and etched illustrations. Only very few photographs appeared. The Danish fashion magazines *Dagmar* and *Nordisk Mønster-Tidende* published pictures of fully clothed women only, and corsets and other underwear were shown as loose items of clothing, not on a woman's body. Advertisements for corsets in newspapers and periodicals in Britain and France, such as *Lady's Pictorial* and *Les Modes*, were also often illustrated only with drawings of fully dressed corseted women.

On 11 December 1900 Duzaine Hansen opened a small exhibition of corsets in his shop in Copenhagen. It consisted of twenty-six very attractive French corsets bought at the World Exhibition in Paris. The exhibited corsets were admired by many and written about in the press. The following appeared, for example, in the press the next day:

Experienced people will have noticed that over the past few days an ever-increasing number of the daughters of Eve have found their way up the small steps leading to Duzaine Hansen's corset shop in Östergade. But this is because

Duzaine Hansen's first photograph of a female model wearing a heavily boned corset. It was not published at the time because it was considered too risqué.

Elegant corset from Duzaine Hansen bought at the Exhibition Universelle in Paris, 1900. Made of pale blue satin bands, it has an attractive lace border at the top and broad belt effect on the hips.

a number of Parisian corsets, the like of which have never been seen before in Denmark, are on show there. In the face of such exquisite works of art, the strict warnings of doctors are probably in vain.[4]

The most expensive of the Parisian corsets was a gold-embroidered white silk corset at 500 francs. Another was made of white satin with colourful hand-embroidered butterflies. But there were also brightly coloured ones, including a canary-yellow silk corset with black lace trimmings. All the models had busks and agraffes set with artificial stones.

The corset had become, as we have seen, more tightly laced and more decorative than previously, as if the suffering involved in wearing it could be outweighed by making it more attractive and seductive. But why did the corset become tighter and more seductive in this final phase of its life?

The corset was initially a social symbol of the aristocracy, but in the 1830s, after a brief period of absence, it was reintroduced by the wealthy middle classes. The woman's clearly corseted figure and expensive and impractical dress demonstrated her own and her husband's social position; it was also a symbol of physical control and self-discipline, attitudes that were fundamental to middle-class views and the whole way of life of that century. The physical silhouette altered during the nineteenth century in

step with changes of style and fashion, but throughout it all the narrow, corseted waist was the focal point of the female figure.

From around 1876 to 1882, between two periods with bustles, dresses became very slender; the bust, waist and hips were accentuated more than previous fashions had allowed. The rounded female forms, under the control of a corset, were shown in a daring and sensual way, in contrast to the Victorian image of the ideal woman whose posture was supposed to express virtue. The restrictive sexual morality of most of the nineteenth century did not forbid women to make themselves attractive – since this was in fact more or less essential if they hoped to marry and be provided for – but the prevailing sense of morality did not allow women to show any form of sensuality, either in behaviour or in dress.

There were clearly defined norms that divided women into various degrees of respectability: from established married women, through *demi-mondaines* or courtesans – kept women who could attain high social status but who never became respectable – down to street prostitutes. There were no barriers to movement between the latter two groups. In his novel *Nana* Emile Zola writes about the woman of that name who uses her sex appeal to conquer any number of men and ruthlessly exploits their desire in her struggle for luxury and power:

So Nana became the toast of Paris, the queen of first-class tarts, battening on the stupidity and beastliness of males. In the smart world of amorous intrigue, a world of reckless extravagance and brazen exploitation of beauty, her rise to fame was meteoric; and she immediately joined the ranks of the most expensive. Her photo was on display in every shop-window; her name featured in the newspapers. When she drove along the boulevards in her carriage, everyone turned to look and breathed her name like subjects greeting their monarch while she, in her loose dress ... would sprawl back giving a cheerful, friendly smile with her red, painted lips ... She set the fashion; great ladies copied her.[5]

Well-known actresses and *demi-mondaines* played an increasingly prominent role as exponents of new fashions, and this undoubtedly helped to push back the boundaries of what was considered respectable dress.

Until the 1880s, white cotton or linen underwear and a light-coloured drill or linen corset were the symbols of respectability for women. Only *demi-mondaines* and other loose-living women wore coloured or sexy underclothes, which were their 'working clothes'. These kept women had special rights that allowed them to wear daring and seductive clothes because, as moral deviants, they operated outside the social norms of

Corset with long, curved busk and a great number of close-sitting bones, *c.* 1880.

respectability. They were sex objects for men and were despised by virtuous wives, those guardians of morality.

In itself, the light-coloured rather coarse corset, almost without adornment, was not an aesthetic object: it was designed to adapt the body to the current ideal of beauty. But from the end of the 1880s the corset became thoroughly decorative; in addition to the meanings that were already inherent in it, it acquired a completely new aesthetic function.

The close-fitting fashion of around 1880 gave advance warning of an incipient revolt against restrictive sexual morality and puritanical attitudes to the body; but several other phenomena altered attitudes to the body and led to the reduction of moral barriers.

The Industrial Revolution swept throughout Europe in the course of the nineteenth century from its beginnings in Britain, which had led the way in mechanized production. Clothes became cheaper to make and demand for mass-produced goods increased. At the same time there was a rapid population increase in the cities, which led to the rise of a growing urban proletariat. Many women from this group found work in industry or in the various craft industries that still dominated production.

Gradually many unmarried middle- and upper-class women started to earn their own living and become financially independent, but in areas in which they were not socially degraded. A married woman's place was in the home. The new means of production and the greater financial freedom of women led to a changed pattern of consumption; many more people had the opportunity to buy fashionable clothes and other consumer items which would otherwise have been restricted to the upper classes. The cutting of a corset was complicated, but with improvements in technique, the invention of the sewing machine in 1850 and other innovations, it became possible to produce good, inexpensive corsets which women other than those of the upper classes could afford.

The corset did not disappear with the other symbols of social class, as normally happens when a fashion ideal becomes popular with many people. The tight corset was not primarily a fashion phenomenon, as its long lifetime proves. The corseted female body had many other meanings connected with public attitudes to the body and the moral values of the dominant class, and as such it was not easy to get rid of.

In the 1890s the arguments against heavy corseting, voiced most vociferously by doctors and reformers, developed into an out-and-out controversy. But fashion has never been sensible or natural, unless that was what it set out to be. The corset was not abolished, for it conformed to the prevalent ideals of the day; instead it was partly transmuted into a new form of expression which signalled new meanings. The corset became tighter and more decorative than ever before, maintaining its

Elegant French brocade corset with attached suspenders, 1902.

capacity to provide a distinction between the classes by its degree of tightness and of decoration.

Around 1902 the corset achieved an extreme and even more harmful form, probably because of signs that a change of style was imminent: extreme forms tend to arise at the end of a style period. The extravagant hairstyles and dresses of the late Rococo are examples of this tendency.

The alteration in the corset clearly had a social motivation. At the same time the corset became an aesthetic object, although it would not have done so if this had not conformed with the ideals of the time. An important impulse towards making the corset and other underclothes more elegant was the impact of the aesthetics of the Belle Epoque, which started around 1890 and lasted until about 1914. With it came a reaction to the industrial production of decorative art, which mostly consisted of imitations of earlier styles, producing a confused mish-mash lacking in originality. An international movement arose whose aim was to promote quality craftsmanship instead of industrial products and to promote aesthetic product development. One of the movement's central figures was the Englishman William Morris. His theories about the need to build an appreciation of beauty in art (especially decorative art) into social upbringing and education received international attention. Morris tried to apply his ideas to women's dress by creating a beautiful, body-friendly dress that did not rely on a corset to create its shape, but the time was not yet

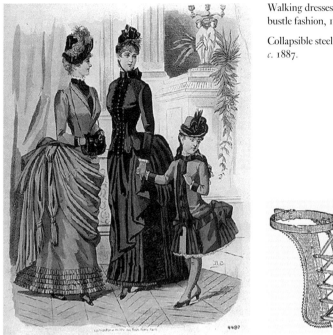

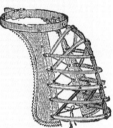

Walking dresses, French bustle fashion, 1884.

Collapsible steel bustle frame, *c.* 1887.

ripe for this attempt at reform and the dress was worn only by the women in his own circle.

The bustle made a return from 1882 to 1888 in an even more extreme form than in its first appearance (*c.* 1870–75). Women wore a crinolette or semi-crinoline outside their corset and underskirt; this was attached at the waist and its frames varied greatly in length and shape. One of the more inventive bustles had a collapsible framework of steel hoops, which was very convenient when women sat down. The dress itself was skilfully draped over the framework, the draperies bearing a strange resemblance to those found in the interiors of contemporary homes!

The female shape of the 1890s was tall and slender, with a raised bust, a very stiff and constricted body, a narrow, corseted waist and a bell-shaped lower half. The look was accentuated by hair that was worn high up on the head, by high-shouldered sleeves, either narrow or leg-of-mutton sleeves which narrowed at the elbow, and by high-heeled shoes. The contrast between day and evening dress became more marked. Day dress consisted mainly of a tailored jacket and skirt with a blouse. Evening dress was extremely decorative.

It became fashionable to wear elegant underwear. Underskirts became especially attractive. Two underskirts at most were worn, but they were usually made of taffeta or silk and richly decorated with frills and lace.

The seductive rustle of the silk skirts as the women walked gave rise to the term 'frou-frou'. The fascination with this sound and the occasional glimpse of a woman's leg when she had to raise her skirt acted as stimulants to the male imagination, which has always found the partly clothed body more erotic than the naked one.

Around 1900 women's underwear consisted most commonly of a chemise, a corset, a corset cover, knickers and underskirts. Some women also wore combinations: these were knickers and chemise combined into one less bulky item. The thin silk and crêpe de chine fabrics now being used for lingerie reduced the weight of underwear still further.

With the introduction in 1902 of the new corset with a vertical busk, the S-shape once more became fashionable, conforming, with its accentuated curves, exactly with the curved ornamentation of Art Nouveau. This style had developed around the end of the 1880s and reached its height around 1900. One of its proponents was the Belgian architect Henry van de Velde, a pupil of Morris who in a way continued Morris's ideas and demands for the creation of sensible and attractive products. But whereas Morris rejected industrial production, van de Velde tried to create an industrial art to be appreciated on its own terms. This style became known as Art Nouveau or in its German form as Jugendstil.

Like Morris, van de Velde also made several suggestions for the reform of clothing. His designs for wide, loose dresses, decorated with the sinuous ornamentation of Art Nouveau, were based on quite different principles from those that determined the curvaceous, corseted feminine ideal that prevailed from about 1902 to 1909. The exaggeratedly artificial form of the latter clearly indicated, however, that the tight corset had entered the last phase of its life.

The ideal feminine shape conformed to the tastes and manners of the time, but how did real women as the recipients of the image relate to this feminine ideal? Women did not agree among themselves about the necessity of wearing a corset; indeed many probably wished to liberate themselves from it.

Through their upbringing and education, middle-class girls were socialized into the role of preparing to make a 'good marriage', which was their only means of leading a successful life. But this custom did not take account of the fact that many women did not get married – there was after all a great surplus of women – and were therefore doomed to becoming 'old maids' and to being supported by their family. Unmarried women could make a living by becoming, for example, governesses or lady's companions, but they never achieved what society believed was their real destiny as wives and mothers; as a result, many of these women had rather unfortunate lives, as accounts of the time testify.

Combinations in silk jersey with
lace borders and shoulder straps,
1902.

Advertisement for 'The Spécialité
Corset' with straight-fronted
busk, 1902.

Elegant walking dress
with short jacket and
bell–shaped skirt, 1905.

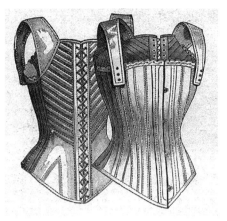

Corset with back
supports for 12–13-year-old girls,
1898.

Dresses for girls,1884. The girl's
dress in the centre has a narrow
corseted waist.

'Le Corset Thylda'. So-called
French 'hygienic corset' with
straight front, broad lace edging
and attached suspenders, 1908

Thit Jensen, a Danish writer and campaigner for women's rights, described how meeting one of these 'old maids' played a decisive role in her desire for independence:

The fourteen-year-old girl was on a visit with her mother to one of the city's grand matrons, a broad, vigorous and authoritative woman. A grey, round-shouldered shadow slipped past and went into a narrow room behind the elegant garden room. Unforgettable. My first sight of an 'old maid'. One of the unfortunate, unmarried members of the family who were graciously allowed to exist; quiet, humble, helpful creatures who sometimes took their own life because, as one said, they had become 'a little odd'. These shadows could be seen in many homes; I will never forget that sliding attempt to make herself invisible to the matronly lady of the house, upon whom God had let his grace shine and given her a husband. There was a gulf fixed between their conditions.[6]

It is hardly surprising, then, that women put on corsets, those instruments of torture, in order to live up to the ideal of beauty and thereby increase their chances in the struggle for a suitable husband. Girls were tied into corsets from an early age to give them an upright posture, a good figure and the coveted slender waist. In this way the muscles of the body and the spine grew accustomed to the artificial support throughout childhood and, to a degree, this did in fact make the corset essential in

adulthood.[7] For everyday use, girls could get away with a less stiffened bodice, buttoned or clasped at the front, but for balls or special occasions a corset was essential if the dress was to fit as fashion dictated.

Although the daughters of the middle class gradually received better education, which in turn opened doors to alternatives to marriage, the latter was still regarded as the best option for a woman and a sign of her success. Married upper- and middle-class women did not have paid work. In middle-class family ideology, the woman's place was in the home and it was the man's duty to support his family as befitted his station. The home was the physical framework for the middle-class family and here the woman was the central figure. It was her duty to organize home life: apart from housekeeping, bringing up the children and care of the family, the wife also had the important role of ensuring that the home presented the right public face and that the rules of etiquette were observed. Her own personal behaviour and dress were the ultimate evidence of her husband's social position and their level of cultivation. Dressed in tasteful, fashionable clothes which accentuated her corseted figure, she not only demonstrated her husband's wealth, but also embodied middle-class ideals.

Many younger women wanted to liberate themselves from the corset and the restricted sexual role it symbolized, but the older generation of women held on to their corsets as an expression of the traditional attitude to the body. Edith Rode was born into the upper middle classes of Copenhagen in 1879 and experienced the 'corset controversies' of the 1890s. As a young girl she tried to avoid the tight corset that convention dictated be worn under her ball gown:

'My child,' said grandmother firmly, 'you must at least wear your corset to the ball!'

'I can't breathe,' I said defiantly.

'I can breathe,' said grandmother, 'your mother can breathe, and your sisters can breathe – and you can breathe, too! . . . It is unfitting and disreputable not to wear a corset . . . And where would you have the young man place his arm, if I may ask?'

'Well, she's wearing a bodice,' my mother said, hurt.

But grandmother was unperturbed. 'A bodice!' she scoffed. 'He can't place his arm on a bodice!'[8]

Edith Rode cast off her corset and bought a new-style dress with matching underwear, all of which hung from the shoulders instead of being tied at the waist – not because she thought it was attractive, but as a protest against the arch middle classes. Yet when her grandmother said that girls looked pusillanimous in 'reform' dresses, she quietly put it away. Something more than a desire for reform was needed if one wanted to move outside the aesthetic norms.

Body and clothes have collaborated not only to emphasize the prevalent ideal but also to demonstrate opposition to established ideals. The struggle of women to achieve equality in male-dominated society has in various ways been expressed in a form of dress or appearance that deviates from the established norms, usually by making them look more masculine. The impotence and subordinate role of women have meant that they have had to conform to the established norms and conventions but have been unable themselves to influence them.

In the middle-class era of the nineteenth century, the social position of women was reduced. Clothes and personal decoration increasingly became women's special area of expression, not because women were less able to express themselves verbally, but because patriarchal society found it natural to set narrow limits for women's field of activity. Freedom to realize themselves could lead to the loss of the essential aspect of 'female nature' – their extremely precious femininity.

Agitating for women's liberation, Georg Brandes wrote:

We treat our women's minds as the Chinese treated their women's feet and as the Chinese did, we perform this operation in the name of beauty and femininity. A woman whose feet have been allowed to grow to their natural size appears to a Chinese man, and especially a Chinese woman, to be unfeminine and unattractive. A freely developed woman is thought in our petty bourgeois China to be an unattractive and unfeminine freak and the stupidity of our best authors and poets has faithfully defended and approved the judgement of the bourgeois masses.[9]

The women's movement was given greater weight with the publication of John Stuart Mill's book *The Subjection of Women* in 1869. It fully recognized the right of women to equality and supported the argument that freedom should be for all, not just for men. Mill wrote that women had put up with a subordinate role and had not demanded equality for too long. They had not packed their bags and left in protest against the tyranny, because from childhood they had been brought up to behave nicely, to please others and to deny themselves. The most deep-rooted fault in women was their desire to please: to be beautiful to look at and conditioned in their manners. Mill pointed out that the subordinate social position of women was an exceptional breach of the basic principles of modern society and that it was a consequence of men's deep fear of being bested by women – they knew perfectly well that women were their equals.[10]

John Stuart Mill's book was an unreserved defence of the female sex. But women did not achieve equal rights just because a few men exposed the injustice of their oppression: it was the hard struggle of women themselves that gradually won victories, some greater, some smaller, along the road to equality.

The first organized women's movement started in the USA in 1848 when a public meeting was called by Elizabeth Cady Stanton at Seneca Falls to work out a programme for women's rights. American women had expected to be given the right to vote as early as the Declaration of Independence in 1776, but this was blocked. The declaration of human rights in the French Revolution of 1789 was also based on the principles of liberty and equality, but these rights did not extend to women either. The Code Civile Napoléon of 1804 completely disbarred women from taking any part in public life.

The American women's rights movement, which later caught on in Britain and then in other countries in Europe, was initially focused on the right to vote and later on the improvement of the condition of women in other areas. One of the first points on the programme was the introduction of sensible and comfortable dress and the abolition of the corset, the harmful effects of which on the body had been the subject of heated debate, especially since around 1850.

The American journalist and feminist Amelia Jenks Bloomer (1818–94) is known as one of the first reformers of dress. In 1849, together with some other women, she started one of the first magazines to support the women's movement, *The Lily*, becoming its editor and later its owner. At the beginning of 1851 *The Lily* presented her proposal for reformed dress; it consisted of long, Turkish-style trousers worn with a knee-

Amelia Jenks Bloomer in loose trouser dress of her own design, 1851.

length, loose tunic – and, of course, no corset. The outfit caused debate because trousers were regarded by most as unseemly and ridiculous for women. Amelia Bloomer wore the outfit herself when she travelled round giving lectures on women's liberation and equal rights in society. If women wanted to achieve the same rights as men, she argued, they would have to get rid of their impossible dress.[11] The Bloomer dress, as it became known, never became very popular as a form of everyday clothing. It was worn only by a group of feminists and dress reformers – the so-called Bloomer Movement, which emerged in several places in the 1850s. On the other hand, this style of trouser dress was used as gym clothes for girls when physical exercise was introduced into the school curriculum at the end of the nineteenth century.

In the 1860s four women doctors held a series of lectures in Boston dealing with the crippling effect of modern women's dress. The corset, with its tight lacing, constricted the ribcage and waist and thus caused considerable damage to the internal organs and reduced women's freedom of movement.[12] The evidence of these doctors gave added substance and force to the reform efforts of the women's movement.

In the 1880s Rational Dress movements started in Britain and other countries in Europe, with the aim of creating and promoting a comfortable and practical 'reform dress' for women on the same principles as the American doctors had advocated. The idea of the reform was to shift the weight of the clothes and underclothes from the waist and hips to the shoulders and to reduce the weight of underclothes; in addition, the corset was to be abolished and replaced with an elasticated bodice. However, despite all efforts to create a reform dress that could compete with fashionable dress, and even though the efforts were followed up by lectures and health campaigns, the costume never became popular. Only a very few emancipated women ignored the sartorial norms and wore it. Most people thought reform clothes clumsy and they were often called 'reform sacks'.

In an article written in 1895 Dr Otto Rosenbach called further attention to the harmful effects of corset lacing: 'The pressure of the corset is harmful in that it interferes with the body's most important functions (respiration, blood circulation and digestion) by pressing on the organs in the chest and abdomen. In fact, there is now no doubt at all that the frequency of illness amongst young women is the result of wearing a tight corset.'

Dr Rosenbach believed that the increasing incidence of anaemia in women was caused by ever tighter lacing at the chest and abdomen. But he recognized that such warnings fell on deaf ears, 'since there is no law which meets with such blind obedience as the law of fashion'.[13]

Reform dress was anti-fashion dress, an attempt to create an outfit based

Tailor-made outfit consisting of a jacket of masculine design and long skirt. Harrods, London, 1902.

on care for health – something that fashion never does. Reformers hoped that it would be adopted particularly by women of the upper and middle classes, who were the prime wearers of corsets. But most of these women were not 'liberated' – they were in quite a different situation from the so-called 'emancipated' women – and could not wear clothing that was inconsistent with their own self-image.

A number of women gradually gained more influence over their own situation, and began what amounted to a revolt against the prevailing image of femininity. Emancipated women wore masculine clothes to distance themselves from specifically 'female' attitudes, which they believed kept women in a subordinate position: equality could be gained only by eliminating the feminine. The 'tailor-made' – a tailored costume consisting of a jacket and skirt, often worn with a shirt and tie – was a revolutionary form of dress, first worn as a kind of uniform of sexual politics. In the beginning it was criticized as unseemly and unfeminine, but it was also practical and it was quickly adopted by other groups of women. Tailor-mades were worn both by the growing number of working women as working clothes and by the upper classes as smart fashion dress.

Women's fashion drew inspiration from men's clothing, although it included light, high-necked, often very feminine blouses and elegant underwear under the simple costume. The sophisticated combination of masculine and feminine in fashionable dress signified a tendency towards a redefinition of the traditional role of women.

The second half of the nineteenth century was characterized by a confusion of styles. Fashions changed rapidly; there was no longer just one, but several more or less contradictory feminine ideals; and the struggle of women for liberation was fought in several, often mutually militant, directions. It was a period of upheaval in which different interest groups were working to reform women's dress, each of them operating from its own perception of the feminine ideal of the day. Although members of the reform movement and its supporters had cast off their corsets, they did not manage to abolish the corset entirely in fashionable dress: it formed the very basis of the dress and was therefore, most people thought, impossible to get rid of.

Karen Blixen wrote very pertinently about the corset controversy:

I have lived through a time when this question really made the headlines. The newspapers – not only ladies' journals – published articles about it, and the corsetless outfit was called reform dress. But the corsets carried off the victory that time. True enough, there were those who agreed that corsets could be somewhat shorter and looser, but it was impossible for a lady to have a well-dressed appearance without corsets, for how could a dress be made, and how could it fit properly without them? No one was able to answer this question, and corsets grew longer and longer . . . And now, fifteen years later . . . the problem of how to make and fit dresses has been solved, although no one can really explain what actually brought this about.[14]

The corset was not abolished for health reasons or because the aesthetic norms were rejected; instead, the feminine ideal underwent alteration as a result of several convergent tendencies. An important factor in the struggle for women's emancipation and for physical liberation in particular was the growing popularity of sport. The practice of sport, like the walking dress, first became popular in Britain, but spread rapidly to the rest of Europe.

Women started to take up sport in earnest in the 1890s – especially cycling and tennis – and for this practical clothing was needed. Women initially cycled in long skirts and tight corsets, but it soon became obvious that trousers were the only really practical thing. Women started wearing baggy trousers of the same style as the 'bloomers' they had previously rejected, and a long-tailed jacket, ignoring the fact that they were regarded as frivolous and unfeminine. There is a clear warning against putting 'femininity' at risk in Professor Frantz Howitz's attack on women cyclists:

I shall not tarry long with bicycling; that it is unhealthy for women, especially when strenuous, must be obvious, but it is to be hoped and expected that the good sense and taste of our women will mean that this unattractive sport will soon cease, particularly in the case of women.[15]

This statement, in a book called *Contribution to Health Education for Women*, provoked many letters of protest from women, including this one:

The poor sport of cycling is given short shrift by the author who demands beauty. This constant attack on the unattractiveness of this sport cannot but just as constantly make us rejoice, since we must assume that the eternal tendency of our sex to please the brave men who placed us and the demand for beauty so high must in the end contribute to teaching us to cycle calmly and respectably.[16]

In another article, 'On Cycling for Women', Marie Luplau wrote:

A number of voices have been raised at home against women's cycling; I do not mean the voices of the indignant who think it unfeminine, unseemly, etc., they will be silenced of themselves; it is only a question of time ... I mean those voices that come from doctors and others, partly supportive, but worried persons who see a danger to health in women's cycling.

I spoke one day with a lady who declared that she felt 'dreadfully ill' after cycling five miles. She was wearing a corset.[17]

Wearing a tight corset during a sporting activity was positively dangerous and many tales were told of the accidents it had caused. Instead of adding to the pressure to abolish the corset, which was not considered a serious option, this merely fuelled moves to stop women cycling. Nevertheless, a rational bodice or a looser corset was recommended for sport, made either of linen with elastic gussets or of soft jersey, with just a couple of stays at the front and the back to give the figure the required support without damaging the internal organs.

Gradually people became accustomed to seeing women cyclists in their practical cycling clothes. Perhaps not all of them looked smart, but they could move relatively freely and this was something new for women.

Physical exercise, first introduced into schools and later practised at colleges and sports associations, had the same liberating effect on the body; wearing a loose gymslip, women could use their bodies in a completely new, active way. But many doctors, including Professor Howitz, expressed concern that too much hard exercise could be dangerous, especially for adolescent girls who had started to menstruate.[18]

Sport had a greater influence on women's dress than the appeals from reformist women. Sport encouraged the development of a new attitude to the female body and this in turn had an effect on the ideal images produced from around 1910. The aesthetic body ideal now became a healthy, supple and well-cared-for body.

The women's liberation movement affected all levels of society. Women became visible for the first time in ways other than as representatives of the feminine ideal. They set their own goals, were self-confident and wore

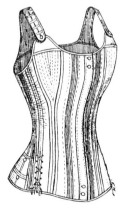

Cycling outfit with jacket and divided skirt, 1901.

Advertisement for a smart cycling outfit with baggy trousers – 'bloomers' – *c.* 1900.

Rational bodice, lightly stiffened, recommended for sports and working wear, 1903.

masculine items of clothing which, naturally, caused a great deal of criticism. It was not only men who expressed their anxiety about what the women's movement might bring in its wake: many women of the older generation were also critical of women's emancipation and many newspapers and magazines poked fun at it; the British magazine *Punch* carried many satirical cartoons of women's struggle for equality. The attempts of

English suffragettes campaigning for the vote, c. 1903.

feminists to redefine their previously restricted role were made to look ridiculous and they were depicted with 'unattractive' and 'unfeminine' characteristics; indeed, such terms were applied to any kind of deviation from or break with the established ideals. The British suffragettes and the 'blue stockings', as intellectual women were called, mostly wore slightly masculine, simple and practical clothes, which certainly deviated from the fashion ideal, although today it is difficult to see how they could appear so frightening. Reformist women wore more masculine clothes, not in an attempt to break down gender identity, but to free themselves from the socially created ideals of femininity, which they believed kept women in a subordinate role. Consciously masculine or asexual forms of dress constitute a protest against the production of ideal images and the compulsion they imply.

All the middle-class female roles changed during this period, though not all to the same degree. Women wanted to achieve the same rights as men and greater freedom to pursue their own needs; but conditions were not the same for all women, and this meant that the women's movement embodied a variety of forms of practice and expression.

For the unmarried pioneers of the women's movement it was essential to agitate for better education and business opportunities so that they could create acceptable living conditions for themselves. In some ways – since they were already social pariahs – it was also easier for them to come forward publicly and criticize philistinism and the double standards that were rife at the time.

In 1879 Henrik Ibsen's *A Doll's House* had its première and in 1883 Bjørnstjerne Bjørnson's play *A Glove* was staged. Both of these plays by

Norwegian writers caused a storm by demanding equality between married partners and the same sexual morality for men and women. Their discussion of the emancipation and equality of women contributed to a heated debate about sexuality. In Denmark in 1885 provocative articles by Arne Garborg and Georg Brandes advocated a freer attitude towards sex and attacked the ideology surrounding women's chastity, which often led to 'the bigotry of suppressed desires'. The challenge was aimed partly at unmarried women, with their ascetic lifestyle, but also at married couples, particularly over the issue of equal sexual morality. The question was how this latter was to be accomplished. Should women behave like men or should men behave like women in the area of moral conduct? This debate was called the 'morality controversy'.

Much was written about sexuality, a topic that had previously been taboo for women. For the first time women could publicly admit that they had sexual needs, although the extent to which they would be allowed to integrate eroticism into their married lives or to behave as lovers was more uncertain.

The image of the virtuous and respectable woman, the socially created ideal, was still maintained by the many women who did not believe in the liberalization of sexual morality. The attitude of women to sex was often ambiguous: they demanded reserve, but suffered from it. Taboos and prejudices were juxtaposed in the consciousness of women with desires and expectations.

The demand from men for a more liberated sexual morality had, despite opposition, an effect on the role of wife and other female roles. Married women began to assume the role of sexual partner; reproduction and sexuality were no longer so closely connected because of altered moral attitudes and the availability of contraception. A number of women underlined their more liberal morality by, among other things, wearing decorative and seductive underwear.

The elegant and luxurious silk, satin and chiffon underwear characteristic of the first decade of this century was created to be seen. Equally, it expressed a change of attitude among women – a sign of greater self-confidence.

Between around 1903 and 1910 many pattern journals carried a page of reform dresses in almost every issue. These oufits were more attractive than earlier models, but their loose cut still deviated from the fashion ideal that lingered on until about 1910. Then the French designer Paul Poiret's ideas for a lighter and looser form of dress, to suit the then current ideals and lifestyles, became popular. He was not alone: from now on, the new designs were no longer opposed to the dominant style but were an expression of it.

Paul Poiret's new flowing line inspired by Léon Bakst's costumes for the Ballets Russes and by Japanese dress. Drawing by George Barbier.

6 The New Slender Look
c. 1910–29

The new type of dress that became popular around 1910 represented the new feminine ideal, in which attention was drawn away from the bust, waist and hips. This change in the ideal body, from strongly accentuated curves to toned-down lines, did not happen overnight. There were a number of factors that provoked the change.

It was the designer Paul Poiret who first drew together the many currents of thought and preference to develop a revolutionary new style, in many ways breaking with previous principles of form and, most of all, releasing the female body from the laced corset.

In 1909 the Ballets Russes, under the leadership of Serge Diaghilev, visited Paris and inspired Poiret with their distinctive costumes, designed by Léon Bakst, and especially with the freedom of movement these costumes gave the dancers. Poiret created a series of orientally inspired dresses in vivid colours, most of them with a high waist and hanging loosely around the figure; these dresses were received enthusiastically and formed the basis of the loose, flowing line that became the new aesthetic fashion ideal. The style bore many similarities to the high-waisted chemise of the Empire period – a very youthful fashion whose loose cut gave women a feeling of freedom. A slender, youthful and supple body was after all the very epitome of the new feminine ideal.

The idealized wax display mannequins of the period exhibited the slender and youthful ideal body, but their appearance and poses changed throughout the period. Until 1915 they had a naturalistic body, with a softly swelling bust, narrow hips and slightly accentuated waist. This was a feminine ideal – coquettish and posturing – but in contrast to the earlier full-figured type of woman, it was not overproportioned. The figures mostly had real hair and glass eyes. The body was subsequently defeminized until it reached the ideal of the 1920s, which was a straight, boyish shape, totally lacking in curves.

From the mid-1920s the production of mannequins was influenced by the new Art Deco style, the more stylized successor of Art Nouveau. The new style became popular at the 1925 Paris Exhibition, the official title of

Tunic creation with high waist, falling softly around the figure, characteristic of Paul Poiret's new design, 1911.

which was 'Exposition Internationale des Arts Décoratifs et Industriels Modernes'. An exhibition of mannequins in the new Art Deco style opened in Paris in the same year. The hair was moulded and the eyes were painted on. The body was square-set and often a little heavy – the material used could not give the same impression of suppleness as did, for example, the fashion sketches of the time.

It became increasingly common to use mannequins in window displays, but the display of corsets and lingerie in the first ten years of the period was limited to busts. It was not until the 1920s that use of the whole figure became permissible. The display of goods on mannequins had aroused protest right from the beginning, but there was a gradual shift in the taboos surrounding the human body. The first live model shows took place around 1913. These were exclusively for women and even the managers of dress departments were not allowed in. Nevertheless the 'woman shows' aroused great indignation among society's moral guardians, who thought it was not respectable to show clothes on live models to the public. But the shows continued and the indignant voices gradually fell silent.

The ideal body after 1910 did not have a wholly natural figure; instead, another artificial product was created, which sent out a different set of signals. The loose style of dress that now became fashionable made the tight corset redundant. Corsets became lighter and less heavily boned, but they were not generally abolished. Many elderly women, who had worn a corset

Wax mannequin with softly rounded female forms by Pierre Imans, Paris, 1912.

Mannequin by Pierre Imans in chemise and elastic corset with lacing at the back, 1922.

all their lives, thought it unseemly not to have this support and continued to wear heavily boned corsets. Young women mostly wore lightly boned, modern corsets. More elastic fabrics were gradually introduced to mould the body. Poiret called the new elasticated corsets, which sat tightly round the hips, 'body-stockings'. The slender ideal was less tightly constricted at the waist, but required greater support around the hips – it was a rare woman who was as narrow across the hips as the fashion dictated.

Modern corsets were rather low in the bust and went right down over the hips; they had a double busk fastened at the front, laces at the back and suspenders attached at the bottom. This shape was mostly worn under the very narrow skirt fashionable at the beginning of the period. But corsets gradually became shorter. New 'girdle corsets' or 'girdles', appealing to a younger clientèle, were introduced around 1914. Short 'waist-girdles' were produced for young girls and for sports wear.

Modern corset, closely fitting across the hips, 1916.

(top left) Brassière, 1905, in the 'new shape' with attached belt at the waist and straps with hooks to keep underwear in place, front and back views.

(below left) Brassière, 1905, boned, front fastening, shoulder straps with buttons and elastic at the sides.

(far right) 1912 advertisement for 'Der Hautana *Büstenhalter*' without boning. It was made of soft jersey and silk to be worn directly on the body and was fastened with buttons at the back.

The need of women for corsets varied according to age, build and usage:

Ensure you have different corsets for different uses. It sounds extravagant, but it is the most economical solution in the long run. A good-quality, light, pale and expensive corset kept only for special occasions will then last much longer than if it also were used for vigorous activity. In addition, one must have a short, loose corset for sports and work around the house so that one may move about without hindrance.[1]

In the first ten years of the period better-quality corsets were made of brocade or silk, with cotton drill kept for everyday use. White, blue, grey and pink were the most popular colours, often in striped or patterned designs. They were imported from many different countries, but British and American articles began increasingly to dominate the market. The new style of corset moulded the body to the new current ideal. The focus of control was no longer the waist but the hips. However, whereas earlier corsets went right up over the bust and functioned both as a support and to push the bust up or out, depending on what was fashionable at the time, the new corset was low and provided no support at all. So it became more common to wear a brassière, not to accentuate the bust, since that was not the fashion, but for support.

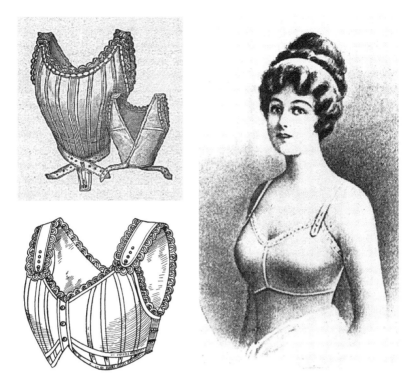

Various types of binding for the bust, for support and adornment, have been known since ancient times, but they were not called brassières. Several new types of 'bust improver' appeared in the 1880s. They consisted of two hemispherical cups, made of woven horsehair over a frame of steel wires or of fabric stiffened with whalebone (celluloid was also used). They were worn over the chemise but under the corset, with a view to creating the prominent bust that was then admired.

The predecessor of the actual brassière appeared around 1890. It had the same shape as a short camisole, but sat close to the body and had whalebone stays inserted to provide a rounded effect. The new article of underwear was called a 'bust bodice' – the name 'brassière' was first introduced in the United States in 1907. The brassière appeared in various forms and was mostly boned, but in 1912 the corsetmaker Sigmund Lindauer patented 'Der Hautana Büstenhalter' without stays. In 1913 Mary Anne Phelps-Jacobs from the USA invented a very simple brassière which separated the breasts naturally: it was made of two silk handkerchieves sewn together, with straps added. The invention was patented under the name Caresse Crosby and was later bought by Warner Brothers Corset Company. But many other models were produced.

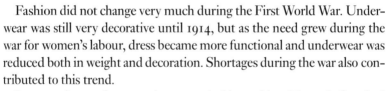

Cover of department store catalogue, 1927, showing contemporary feminine ideal with short hair in loose chemise.

Bust flattener with satin shoulder straps and silk elastic girdle, 1923.

Fashion did not change very much during the First World War. Under-wear was still very decorative until 1914, but as the need grew during the war for women's labour, dress became more functional and underwear was reduced both in weight and decoration. Shortages during the war also con-tributed to this trend.

In 1915 dresses became shorter and skirts wider. Never before had women shown so much of their legs. Again, protests were voiced by female moralists, but neither they nor any of the subsequent demands for 'respectability' could prevent the liberation of the female body: the process had only just begun and in the 1920s it became even more widespread than most people could have imagined.

Towards 1919 the slender dress that reached down to the ankles had become the norm, and underwear consisted of light combinations or a ca-misole and knickers with slender lines. In 1920 many of the knickers were designed with elastic at the waist rather than the earlier ties.

The feminine ideal of the 1920s was a boyish figure, with no visible waist, bust or hips. Emancipated women had a streamlined body without curves and a short, boyish hairstyle. The standard type of dress, a func-tional chemise in which women could move about easily, fell loosely about the body. From 1924 dresses grew gradually shorter until in 1927 they reached the knee. From about 1923 the waistline dropped as far as the hips, drawing attention to their boyish slimness.

Corsets were either lightly boned, often with elastic at the sides and the top, and with a busk at the front, or were made of elasticated material, closed, without laces, stays or busk. This type gradually became known as a roll-on, because, as the name implies, it had to be rolled on. In addition, women wore a tight brassière whose function was neither to support nor to accentuate the bust, but to flatten it. Between around 1910 and 1920 the bust was neither accentuated nor flattened. Female shapes could not, of course, just disappear simply because the ideal body was supposed to be without curves, so some women compressed their bust with a firm bodice or bandeau to achieve the 'correct' shape. The flat bandeau was mostly made of linen, silk or jersey, fastened at the side or with elasticated backs; pink and white were the most popular colours.

A combination of brassière and corset appeared in the USA in 1919 and was called the corselet. It was a slender tube with an unbroken line from the bust to the hips, usually with elastic side panels, shoulder straps, side fastening and no stays. The most commonly used fabrics were cotton-drill and silk. The corselet replaced the body-shaping function of the corset and the brassière as an even more effective way of achieving the coveted boyish look of the 1920s.

Better heating in the home and a more active way of life for women contributed to the evolution of a lighter form of dress and underwear. Combinations were a favourite form of underwear in the 1920s. They were made of coloured crêpe-de-chine, silk or artificial silk and were often decorated with embroidery and lace. But the principal developments in women's clothing between around 1908, when Poiret created a more body-friendly form of dress, and the 1920s, when simple, functional clothing became popular, were mostly connected with the altered position of women in the family and in society. Men's dress did not change to the same degree; the revolution that was underway in women's dress had happened a century earlier in men's dress.

The change in style marked a break with some ideals and values which were no longer in tune with the times and with which the younger generation of women, who had a different attitude to life, could not identify. Poiret's loose style of dress became the new aesthetic expression because it was consistent with the ideals then current. It became a symbol of physical liberation and freedom for women to move into areas that previously had been restricted to men. The new femininity was, therefore, not expressed in an accentuation of the female body but in a toning down of female curves, a trend that became even more pronounced in the boyish body ideal of the 1920s.

Advertisement,
c. 1925, for Twilfit
boneless corselettes
with elastic panels.

Fashion in the 1920s was dominated by female designers, who were more responsive to women's needs. The designer who most clearly made her mark on women's dress of the period was Gabrielle (Coco) Chanel. She started to design clothes before the war, but became better known after 1919 when she opened her own fashion house. Chanel radically changed women's dress by introducing simplicity; she created simple, practical clothes, perfectly suited both to the more active lifestyles of women and to the functional lines of design in other fields of art, craft and architecture. Her rather sporty three-piece outfits, consisting of jacket, skirt and blouse, mostly made of soft jersey, were especially popular. Chanel's clothes tended towards a democratization of fashion by being relatively easy and cheap to copy; but although less material was required for the short, simple dress, most fashion designers used expensive materials for special occasions, extravagantly embroidered with beads and sequins to mark a social difference between the dress of the upper class and that of the other classes.

When most women were employed in agriculture and were suntanned, a pale, delicate complexion had been a sign of wealth. But with the growth of industry in the nineteenth century, many women were employed in factories and shops, often working under very hard conditions, and as a result most working women suffered from poor health and a pale skin.

Among the wealthier sections of society, however, sports and healthy activities became increasingly popular. Physical exercise became an important part of modern body culture and beauty care. Beauty and health became almost synonymous. The fashionable middle classes moved to the country in the summer and took their holidays on the Mediterranean, activities that required time and money. In the process they acquired a suntan. Increasingly during the 1920s, a sleek, slender, tanned body became the social symbol of the upper classes.

Chanel's new style of dress and sports clothes represented a completely new and relaxed manner. Chanel herself led an outdoor life and took part in sports, thus becoming an important exponent of the new style and helping to make a youthful-looking, suntanned body fashionable.

Coco Chanel photographed in 1929 wearing one of her own creations – a simple three-piece in soft jersey.

The feminine ideal of the 1920s was personified in Victor Margueritte's novel *La Garçonne*, published in 1922. The heroine is portrayed as a liberated 'bachelor girl', with a slender, boyish figure and short hair. The 1920s boyish or androgynous look was later called *garçonne* or 'tomboy'. The novel portrays a financially independent and liberated woman who lives a life that is morally and physically equal in every way to that of men – in this case in the modern and somewhat dissolute environment of Paris. Her breaking down of the barriers of acceptability becomes a problem for her only when she falls in love. Women had improved their position in society in many areas, but they had not yet achieved sexual equality. In practice women who led a more liberated sex life were often condemned. In this rejection of traditional femininity inherent in the 'tomboy' ideal of the 1920s, surely it is possible to see a demand for a redefinition of attitudes to women?

'She wishes to be released from her pre-ordained position. She wishes to be a human being before she is a woman. Men have had this right for a long time and have known how to use it. . . . The women's cause will not stop before women have become human beings,' wrote Poul Henningsen in an article in 1935.[2] He considered the increasingly feminine direction that clothing was taking in the 1930s, when women were again expected to think, feel and look like women, as an enormous step backwards for women's emancipation and equality.

The development of the boyish or androgynous feminine ideal of the 1920s happened more quickly than it would have done if women had not been so active in the First World War, performing tasks that had previously been reserved for men. In Britain, under the leadership of Emmeline Pankhurst, the suffragettes agitated in vain for women's suffrage in the years before the war. Suffrage for women over thirty was finally introduced in 1918 and they thereby gained political rights – the greatest victory women had won to date. Women in Germany gained the right to vote in the same year, but several other European countries – for example, France – did not give women the right to vote until after the Second World War

Many women had become self-supporting and financially independent, so even if there was a surplus of women after the war and not all of them could expect to get married, there were now better opportunities to take care of themselves. They did not want to give up the progress they had achieved towards greater freedom and equality. In their dress, their boyish appearance and their whole demeanour, they tried to demonstrate equality between the sexes and to eliminate the sex-specific symbols that had until then kept women in the role of passive sex objects.

'Flat-chested, narrow-hipped and no waist, that's what the ideal woman

Elegant evening gown in white velvet with draping in the back, designed by Vionnet, 1925.

of the 1920s looked like – not attractive. Many women had worked like men during the war and now they wanted to look like men. Brasssières came in to flatten the bust, sometimes so much so that women's breasts were squashed out under their arms,' said André Duzaine Hansen in a newspaper interview in 1958.[3] Many men probably shared Mr Duzaine Hansen's views on the tomboy look, but for many women the change was an expression of liberation.

The legs were in focus from the mid-1920s when short dresses became fashionable. French advertisement for silk stockings, 1928.

Short hair marked in a similar way a break with the conventional perception of femininity and became a symbol of equality. In the 1880s the 'What-we-want-women', an advance group of women's liberationists, had cut their hair and toned down their sexual identity in their dress in order to demonstrate their equality with men. There was greater indignation at their short hair then than in the 1920s – the limits of what was acceptable had moved considerably.

Since the ideal body of the 1920s was sexually indefinable, the face and legs came into focus. From about 1925 short dresses showed more of the leg than before, perhaps because legs were indicative of an active lifestyle. This led to increased production of elegant silk and artificial silk stockings; initially they were mainly flesh-coloured, but later they also appeared in beige and brown shades. The visible, silk-clad legs and the increasing use of cosmetics accentuated a new, sophisticated and more liberated femininity, particularly among younger women who had plenty of optimism and self-confidence. A clash with the morality of older women was thus perhaps inevitable. That women smoked cigarettes, wore make-up and went out without a male companion was regarded by many as a sign of moral decline. There was greater openness surrounding sexuality and this had an effect on sexual morality; among younger people this led to much freer and more companionable behaviour between the sexes than before. This was apparent, for example, on the beach, where young people of both sexes appeared in front of each other quite unembarrassed – to the great indignation of older women who wrote frequent articles to the newspapers to complain about their dissolute behaviour.

Bathing scene from 1900: young girls dressed in respectable bathing costumes and drawers.

The practice of going to the beach really started in the 1890s, when the wealthy middle classes spent the summer in the country to get fresh air and to enjoy the pleasures of the great outdoors. But there were strict moral rules associated with bathing. First of all, men and women were not allowed to bathe together; second, women had to ensure that when changing and bathing their bodies were not visible to men. Women put on respectable bathing dresses and accompanying trousers, shoes and headgear, after which they were conveyed right down to the water's edge in horse-drawn bathing machines. Their bodies remained completely hidden in the water.

After the turn of the century, the bathing dress was replaced by an all-in-one bathing suit, which was better adapted to swimming. When going down to the water, it was now possible to make do with wearing a long robe. The impractical bathing dresses did not disappear entirely, but

The latest bathing costumes, *c.* 1920.

were worn in various styles as more decorative beach clothing right through the 1920s. Beach costumes were especially popular at more fashionable resorts such as Newport, Brighton and Trouville, where people gathered in enormous numbers to see and be seen – but not necessarily to bathe. It was mostly children and young people who went into the water: the ladies sat demurely under parasols and watched over the young girls to make sure that their modesty was not offended.

Around 1908 the jersey bathing costume became popular. It almost completely revealed the natural shape of the body, and thus again gave rise to noisy protests. The older generation of women slowly accustomed themselves to the liberties the younger generation took – but not to these bathing costumes. In 1918 a woman wrote:

Bathing is extremely unattractive. The young girls wear intensely ugly bathing costumes, preferably as tight as possible. Men reveal the most peculiar side of their natures; they look at the bathing ladies through binoculars as if the ladies were appearing on stage and the gentlemen were sitting in the stalls and had some right to study them. And one even sees men who derive amusement from lying in wait to catch a glimpse of young girls as they change.

Bathing is characterised by – let us content ourselves with saying – an astounding lack of discretion. And the fault is not only with the men. Modern girls demonstrate a surprising degree of liberality towards the audience that flocks to the beaches. They show themselves in low-necked, sleeveless and very short jersey costumes in front of a whole crowd of people they often know only superficially . . .

It is as if the informality of a bathing costume brings down the whole tone . . . What we lack in bathing is two things: 'tact and a sense of beauty'.[4]

Between 1908 and 1925 protests were heard all over the Western world from moral guardians and other opponents of modern bathing costumes. These were framed in terms of decency and aesthetics, but it was probably more the exposure of the body and its 'naturalness' that aroused their indignation rather than the lack of beauty in the body or in the garments that clothed it. The condemnation would probably have been milder if all the jersey-clad women had conformed with the ideal of beauty!

By around 1925, women's dresses had been shortened to knee length and concealed little more of the female body than did contemporary bathing costumes. People who had been offended by the latter now complained about women's attire generally and about emancipated femininity in particular. The writer Emma Gad was more sober in her advice to bathers. She wrote:

A young woman should guard against splashing about in the briny waves in the company of an admirer. There are really very few people who look their best when bathing. Rather go bathing with girlfriends. Their feelings do not grow cooler just because they see someone less attractive than themselves. Quite the reverse.[5]

Emma Gad had a sense of humour and gave lots of sensible and clear advice in her book, but she belonged to that generation of women who had grown up believing that an attractive appearance was decisive if one

Practical jersey bathing suit, 1922.

'Red Diving Girl', launched by Jantzen Bathing Suits in 1920, symbolized the feminine ideal of that decade: slender, youthful and sophisticated.

wanted to make a good marriage, and that it was therefore important to make the most of one's attributes. Many younger women could support themselves and had achieved a greater degree of social freedom; they did not tolerate being forced to accept society's conventional demands of femininity in order to get a husband.

The feminine ideal of the 1920s was liberated, sophisticated and self-confident, but in practice the question of women's liberation remained more of a problem, especially for married women. The fact that modern young women had become more liberated was tolerated – in line with the reforming spirit of the day – but the place of the married woman was still in the home and it was difficult to reconcile the role of housewife and mother with the struggle for liberation.

The writer and social critic Poul Henningsen's provocative cultural criticism in the 1920s and 1930s dealt with many aspects of behaviour; it also took the form of a defence of a number of democratic and human rights, for example in the area of sex and the women's cause. He wrote:

We have come so far that unmarried women are, in some spheres, equal to men. They have become comrades and that is perhaps the most valuable advance in the relationship between the sexes. This has led to greater sexual equality and must gradually also lead to financial equality. But we have not yet achieved equality for married women. When a woman gets married, when society has used all the means at its disposal to bind her, when she has been tempted by the apparently superior position of being a married woman, and has become an unpaid housekeeper for life, she has gone from being a free human being to being an appendix to the man who keeps her.[6]

The modern liberated woman cultivated in the 1920s expressed herself in many areas other than the erotic; she had become man's friend and she could go on equal terms to most places a man could go. It is impossible to tell how far sexual liberation actually went for women. The sexual revolution of the 1920s was a reaction against the restrictive, condemnatory sexual morality of the Victorian period and the middle-class, conservative forces that still demanded strict moral conduct from women. Many younger women wanted sexual equality; they wanted to have a freer and better sex life without being subject to the many taboos that were set up in the name of decency, but there were hardly any women – and certainly no married women – who had a wild and unrestrained sex life.

The position of women in the family and in society had altered radically during the second decade of the twentieth century: it was a change that had an effect on all areas of a women's lives, but not all women agreed on the value of the progress that went with liberation. The passing of laws on equal opportunities was an improvement for everyone, but many married women thought that the role of the self-supporting woman was being idealized to the detriment of the roles of housewife and mother, both of which they saw as a woman's most noble duty. The most common attitude – not, however, shared by all young women – was that young girls should work only until they got married. Many conflicts arose between the various groups of middle-class women, partly between younger and older women and partly between housewives and women who supported themselves.

Many women's societies worked to support the right of married women to work. This was especially necessary during the crises of the 1930s; but the question of housekeeping became an important issue and, by helping to establish schools for domestic science, for example, an attempt was made to raise the work of women in the home to the same status as work outside the home. Whether married women should work outside the home was the subject of a discussion that went on for many years, but in practice it was controlled by the needs of the labour market for women employees.

The feminine ideal of the 1920s was youthful, liberated and had sex appeal. Beauty was no longer synonymous with a pretty face and a well-proportioned body. The modernistic ideals of the time and the desire of women for freedom both had an influence on the perception of beauty and on the formulation of the ideal of beauty. A slender, boyish body combined with sensuality and emancipation characterized the ideal of beauty. The toning down of female contours and the increasing use of cosmetics were both expressions of liberation. Both of these things helped to change the general perception of femininity and tended towards a subjectivization of women.

Tango dancers, 1927.

The economic and cultural developments that were well underway in the United States finally began to make themselves felt in a number of European countries around 1925–9. The boom affected the way of life and the consumer habits in these countries, although 'Americanization' was most clearly manifested in dance and music. The music and dance of a given culture have always been in tune with the form of dress and the prevalent attitudes to the body. The Spanish–Argentinian tango came to Europe in 1911 and at the same time dress became looser and allowed greater freedom of movement. Jazz music and the hectic Charleston became popular in the 1920s when dresses were shorter and there were

Josephine Baker in her banana skirt, 1926

even greater opportunities for self-expression. Black American music and dance spread quickly, presumably because their spontaneity was in tune with the freedom-seeking aspirations of the time. In return, the interest of whites in black culture led to a greater self-confidence among blacks and to a perception that brown skin was attractive. In 1925 the West Indian dancer Josephine Baker appeared on stage in Paris dressed only in a banana skirt, arousing both fascination and indignation. With her short hair, brown skin and supple body, Josephine Baker expressed a youthfulness and sensual femininity that were totally in tune with the liberated feminine ideal of the time.

The spread of feminine ideals gained a new dimension and greater impact with the arrival of the movies. The film media created types or 'stars' to take films out to the audience. Film stars became exponents of female beauty and the objects of a new type of idolatry. Film producers launched them with advertisements and press releases and marketed them in exactly the same way as any other product. The aim of this publicity was not to demonstrate the acting ability of the stars but to concoct shining dream images for general consumption. Personal qualities such as beauty and charisma were valuable assets in this glittering world and helped to create the idealized image that the audience formed of the star in question and wanted to see when they went to the cinema. Film critic and author Harald Engberg said of this phenomenon:

Greta Garbo, 1929.

Louise Brooks with her black pageboy hair and irresistible charisma was one of the great film stars of the 1920s.

Stars must not be what they are, but what the audience wants them to be. If producers change the way stars are expected to be, you can see the result in box-office sales. So a star is doomed to play his or her one role until the bitter end, until that fund of youth, charm and novelty which made him or her popular has been used up and the audience look around for a new attraction, a new type. This is why stars such as Joan Crawford, Marlene Dietrich, Loretta Young and 'jungle girl' Dorothy Lamour have had to play the same role in film after film. We want them to be like that. They have to be the half mythical person their manager has built up with his pictures and press releases.[7]

This phenomenon was particularly evident in American silent movies. The Swedish actress Greta Garbo was one of those stars and dream women who had their greatest success in the silent movies of the 1920s. She made her debut in a Swedish film called *Luffar-Petter* in 1922, but left for Hollywood in 1925. Here, her cool beauty and sensual femininity quickly created her an image as the beautiful and mysterious sphinx of the films. Garbo played many of her female roles with an edge of dual sexuality, an interplay of masculine and feminine characteristics. Her androgynous and sensual aspects fascinated the film-going public and they were also enthralled by her distinctive beauty. She was difficult to place as a type. Even though her figure and presence represented the modern woman, she avoided any kind of pigeonholing. The ideal image of Garbo has remained intact along with the myth she created around herself, whereas Garbo the person was hidden in loneliness. Roland Barthes wrote that Greta Garbo's beauty could not be changed in the eyes of others – her face had for all eternity to have the one reality that lay in its perfection.[8]

The modern, liberated feminine ideal was made more real and tangible in the person of Louise Brooks, another of the beautiful stars of the silent films of the 1920s. With her black, pageboy hair and strongly erotic aura, she had a beauty that was contemporary and timeless. Louise Brooks's personality, charisma and intensity were most clearly expressed in her German films, when she was directed by Georg Wilhelm Pabst. She had had small roles in Hollywood when Pabst engaged her to play the role of Lulu in his loose interpretation of Frank Wedekind's 1904 play *Die Büchse der Pandora* (*Pandora's Box*) in 1929. In Wedekind's play, Lulu was a destructive monster, but Pabst saw her quite differently: for him, Lulu was the symbol of the emancipated woman who demanded the same right to sexual satisfaction that men had always had.[9]

The film was strongly criticized as immoral and was banned by the censors in several countries. The moralists were well aware of the influence films had on sexual morality and on the perception of women. According to them, the film heroine had to be exemplary and must not contribute to destroying existing ideals and values. But it was not possible then – nor has it been since – to stop the propagation of more serious and socially realistic films which aimed to do more than merely deliver dream images, romance and superficial entertainment.

The film media have taken a central place in cultural life in the same way as theatre, literature, art and music – all of which are expressions of culture that both reflect and are reflected in the spirit of the age – but film is by far the greatest producer of images of the ideal. The modern age is typified by its unlimited production of images that carry meanings. Film in particular has a special talent for creating illusions about reality.

Some films of the time portrayed women's expressions of liberation as the path to moral depravity or as a sign of willingness to comply with the erotic dreams of men. Heroines of the more progressive films of the 1920s, however, showed that emancipation and sex appeal were not the special preserve of 'dangerous' women, but could be combined with a decent way of life.

Photographs of live models also began to appear in magazines in the 1920s. Live models liberated the body in a more direct way than drawings did – not more sensuously, but more physically. The idealized female body of drawn fashion images gives a precise picture of the time. The perfect, but unrealistic, ideal body blends absolutely with the dress in which it is clothed. In the more realistic live model pictures, the body is present in flesh and blood under the clothes, albeit in altered form. It shows what the 'fashionable' body should look like. Photography documents physical authenticity.

Beauty had always been an asset for women, and one that made it possible to make a good marriage. This was still true, but an attractive appearance now also became a business opportunity in itself. Attractive women increasingly appeared as eyecatchers in advertisements – regardless of what was being sold – and the 'right' look could be the key to entry into films and other related media. When the mass media began to make extensive use of pictures of women, beauty became a product.

Beauty contests had started in 1888; the first one took place in the Belgian resort of Spa. The event drew many visitors to the resort and received a great deal of press attention. The nineteen selected beauties, all dressed in evening wear, arrived at the casino with their chaperone and were judged by a male jury. An eighteen-year-old Creole woman from Guadeloupe won the first prize of 5,000 francs. This new form of entertainment and assessment of women's beauty became popular everywhere. Beauty contests were held at many of the fashionable watering holes in the 1920s,

The first beauty contest, held at Spa in 1888. The young woman on the far left won the competition.

The first beauty competition in Denmark, 1 August, 1926, at Marienlyst Beach Promenade near Elsinore.

the young women now appearing in bathing costumes for the judging. The ideal of beauty had changed, but the taboos surrounding the body were also undergoing a complete change. The limits of decency had obviously moved a great deal.

The entire period 1910–29, but especially the second half of it, stands in history as a time characterized by a greater liberalism and a more emancipated feminine ideal compared with the periods immediately before and immediately after it. But in reality, women had only partly achieved the freedom and equality that their dress and their emancipated appearance and attitude to their bodies signalled.

7 The Soft-Contoured, Slender Body
c. 1930–46

There was an obvious change in the feminine ideal in the course of the winter of 1929–30. The economic crisis all over the Western world caused by the Wall Street crash in October 1929 led to unemployment, cuts, anguish and despondency everywhere, which in turn sparked reactionary changes in morality and attitudes to life. This became immediately obvious in fashion and the feminine ideal.

Feminine ideals always clearly express large or small changes in society. In periods of crisis there is a greater need to maintain traditional values; an attempt is made to re-establish some form of order in society and this happens, for example, by underlining sexual identity. The 1920s emancipated tomboy ideal without female curves was replaced in the 1930s by a more feminine ideal. Women were still supposed to be slender, youthful and narrow-hipped, but the waist resumed its natural position and the bust was softly accentuated. The ideal was a slender and 'natural' body.

Mannequins were produced to match this ideal, with bodies that were as natural as possible, given the material of which they were made. The body shape did not alter very much during this period, but the shape of the face and the hairstyles changed around 1940, with variations according to where the mannequins were produced. France had been the leading producer of mannequins until around 1930, but in the 1930s several American factories began to produce mannequins and to compete with the French for the world market.

Attractive wax mannequins no longer dominated. Siégel's studio in Paris had been producing mannequins in sophisticated colours in moulded papier-mâché since the mid-1920s. French mannequins of the 1930s were still inspired by the simple elegance of Art Deco but the geometrical clean lines of Cubism also had an influence. Typically, these mannequins had an oval face with high cheekbones, slightly slanted eyes and finely painted eyebrows, with scraped-back hair and tight curls in the neck or lightly waving hair.

Velvet evening gown by Louise Boulanger, 1931.

Mannequin by Pierre Imans with the characteristic oval face, high cheek-bones and slightly slanted eyes of the 1930s.

Mannequin with soft curves from Siégel's atelier in Paris, early 1930s.

Lester Gaba, the American mannequin producer, often used film stars as models for his 'Gaba Girls'. Marlene Dietrich, Greta Garbo and Carole Lombard were used for this purpose; they were more glamorous than the European models. Danish mannequins were mainly imported from France, but this stopped during the war. Ferdinand Hindsgaul had sole Scandinavian rights to import mannequins from the French company Pierre Imans, and decided to start his own production when the supply dried up during the war. The first model, called Eva, was finished in 1941. Margot and Rita followed, then a couple of male and children's figures. These were a great success in Scandinavia and after the war they were exported to many other countries. Hindsgaul's models had a fresher and more 'natural' appearance and were less heavily made-up than many had been in the 1930s.

The female silhouette of the 1930s was slender and 'natural', but it was a natural look that required some artifice. Care for the body and a good corset to shape it were necessary, but women were not supposed to look as if they were wearing a corset. A 1937 department store advertisement read: 'Modern underwear has one main purpose which puts all others in the shade: to be invisible!' Most advertisements for corsets and fashion reports spoke of the importance of a corset for a woman's well-being: the modern corset gave the figure complete support and fulfilled fashion's demands for slenderness and elegance.

There were several motives behind the massive hype of the feminine ideal: one was, in this period of crisis, to get the growing number of working women to focus more on traditional female attitudes; another was the necessity of underlining the fact that women still needed corsets, even if the ideal was a 'natural' figure. The corset was not supposed radically to alter female curves, merely to correct any 'faults' and keep the figure of the older woman looking youthful and slender.

Live model on the sofa and the new display mannequin launched by Hindsgaul, 1941.

Advertisements in women's magazines appealed to women on the necessity of wearing a corset. A 1939 department store advertisement read:

It can appear quite tempting on a hot summer's day to take off one's brassière, but it is dangerous, very dangerous; only very few busts can do without the gentle support a brassière can give and summer dresses mercilessly reveal flabbiness or defects underneath. The same is true of the girdle or corselette. Only very few women can allow their figures to be quite free.

This kind of pressure made the corset essential for most women. The old type of corset with laces and steel or whalebone supports was not reintroduced: figure control was achieved with the help of new, shaping, elasticated materials. The first elasticated corsets were produced in the USA around 1913. Rubber elastic was used, but the material lost its elasticity relatively quickly and was replaced in 1929 with the newly developed lastex fibres, woven into other fabrics. The development of lastex was a revolution in the corset business and it made American corset manufacturers into world market leaders. Gossard, Warner Brothers and Maidenform were some of the leading brand names. The new corsets were worn directly on the body, like an extra skin that moulded the figure to make it smooth and slender. The new fabrics were easier to wash and personal hygiene improved, largely thanks to sport and the growing cult of health and the body.

The most epoch-making change in underwear was the use of elasticated materials, but the shape of the brassière also altered substantially. In the

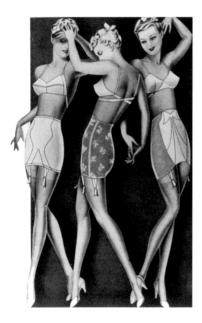

(left) 1939 advertisement for Kesto's corsets and brassières. The model in the picture with elastic straps which cross in the back and are fastened by a button under each breast was one of the most popular styles from the 1930s to the early 1950s.

(opposite) The basis for the silhouette of the dress was still corsetry. Advertisement for Vassarette elastic corselette, 1933.

1920s, its function had been to flatten the bust, but at the beginning of the 1930s it acquired two separate cups, which made it obvious that women have two breasts, a fact obscured by the earlier terms 'bust' and 'bosom'. For most of the 1930s the feminine ideal displayed a 'natural' bust shape and very slender hips in a generally youthful, supple and firm body, achieved with the help of an elasticated corset or corselette.

Dresses fell softly around the figure, following the contours of the body without stiffness in cut or fabric; evening gowns in particular hugged the *(opposite)* Elegant evening gowns with flowing lines which fall softly about the figure, 1933. On the left, a black crêpe-de-chine gown with draped top by Lanvin and on the right, a silk gown with deep back by Patou.

(right) Chiffon evening gown with draped back, smooth hips and full skirt by Vionnet, 1931.

figure closely right down over the hips and from there fell to the floor in soft folds. Short dresses were worn during the day and long dresses in the evening, often cut very low to reveal most of the back. Many dress historians – for example, James Laver – have tried to explain this fixation on the back with the theory that when legs lost their attraction as a focus of erotic interest in the 1930s, attention moved to the back.[1] A characteristic feature of fashion has been the concealment or accentuation of various parts of the female body; as a rule the naked body has been regarded as having less erotic potential than the body that is partly clothed. When, for example, women began to show more of their legs in the 1920s, they were no longer felt to be as sexually exciting as they had been when they were hidden. The accentuation of the legs was more connected with sexual ambiguity and a breaking down by women of sexual barriers. Similarly, the naked back of the 1930s was not perhaps erotic in itself but, by adding further sophistication to the body-hugging dresses, it helped to hint at a new female sensuality. The strict morality of the time did not permit bold or provocative clothing, nor did the women themselves wish to be presented as sex objects; the female fashion designers who dominated Parisian *haute couture* in the 1930s understood how to transform this mood into a toned-down but still exciting and elegant style of dress.

One of the designers who most set her mark on dress style in the 1930s was Madeleine Vionnet. She specialized in cutting her model clothes completely on the bias and used soft fabrics such as crêpe-de-chine, jersey and silk velvet which gave the body-hugging softness and attractive flowing line characteristic of the fashion of the period. Vionnet created simple and functional clothes for women, but the bias cut meant that her styles, unlike those of Chanel, were not suitable for copying – this was tailoring for the upper class.

One feature characterized the softly draped dresses of the 1930s: they were all tight and smooth across the hips and this area was often accentuated with sophisticated cuts or folds. The feminine ideal was very markedly feminine – both the clothes and the posture of the models in fashion and women's magazines were youthfully feminine and very graceful – apart from the hips, which were flat and almost boyishly narrow. The corset shaped and flattened the hips and, in its new guise, it was still the foundation for the shape of the dress.

The 1930s corset was produced in many different models and fabrics, but almost exclusively in tea-rose, rose-beige or salmon pink colours. One of the most popular models had wide inset gussets in silk elastic and elastic at the waist; it had spiral wire supports sewn in and a front busk. The same model was produced with a zip or catches at the side. Brocade, satin drill and patterned silk batiste were among the most popular fabrics.

1941 advertisement for the popular Lift brassière with stitched and lace cups and a broad belt.

Roll-ons and lastex corsets in tube form were a lighter type of corset mostly worn by young women and under summer clothes. They were made either of elasticated tulle or lastex combined with lace, tulle or silk. A girdle with a matching brassière in tea-rose silk was introduced for young girls.

Most brassières at the beginning of the 1930s were made of tricot charmeuse in a soft form which did nothing other than provide support, but they gradually became stiffer and provided more shape. A very popular brassière that became almost the epitome of the 1930s brassière was the Lift. Advertising copy from 1938 reads:

The Lift system, with its quilted cups, lifts, supports and points the bosom so that it achieves the modern silhouette. The modern models have a lastex gusset which gives a more divided bosom. With Lift, the ideal, the beautiful, high, pointed bustline is achieved.

The bra, as it was now also called, was produced in various sizes and lengths. It was often made of lace and satin silk or satin. The cheaper models were made of satin drill, cotton-twill or brocade.

Modern corsetry was mainly produced in Britain and the USA, which were leaders in the areas of fit and development of new fabrics. But many specialist corset shops still made corsetry of their own design and according to individual needs. Spirella became a large and well-respected corsetry company which specialized in a personal, made-to-measure service. The company was established in Britain at the beginning of the twentieth century and during the first half of the century salons and factories were established in several other countries to produce Spirella corsets. Spirella salons were typically established in large towns and it was

here that ladies could be fitted for a corset and get advice on corsetry and on looking after their figure. The salons could also direct customers to the nearest trained Spirella corsetière, who came to the customer's own home by appointment to take measurements. Spirella came to stand for well-made and well-fitting corsetry, and claimed in their advertising to be the first company to take individual needs into consideration:

We not only produce made-to-measure corsets, but with the aid of our measuring models, we model your figure into its most attractive shape before we take your measurements.

The figure was shaped and idealized before measurements were taken so that an attractive foundation was created for the clothes; in other words, they took the demands of fashion into consideration more than individual needs. Spirella continued in business until the end of the 1960s.

The corselette reshaped the female body in the 1920s to a slender tomboy figure. In its new form, it was ideal for moulding bust, waist and hips into one slim, unbroken, elegant line. The corselette was made of almost exactly the same fabrics as the corset – satin drill for the cheapest, silk batiste for the most expensive; a combination of lastex and tulle or silk was also popular. It had inset elasticated gussets which pulled in the hips, a lace bust and mainly side fastening.

In 1939 the feminine ideal underwent a clear change, as presented in many corset advertisements, most of which consisted of drawn illustrations, rarely a photograph. The decent female type of the 1930s gave way to a more glamorized type with greater sensual appeal and heavier make-up. The corset made the bust higher and more pointed, the waist was more clearly defined and the slender hips became more rounded. This dream girl, promoted alongside and in contrast to the respectable ideal woman, gradually broke down the barriers of taboos and demands for decency, until in 1939 a sexier feminine ideal came to the fore. It was evident in advertisments for the Hollywood Maxwell bra:

Learn from Hollywood's 'Stars'.
Notice that all film stars have that sophisticatedly high bustline. And follow their example: use the famous Hollywood Maxwell Brassière and have a beautiful, firm, youthful bust.

The 'Glamour' brassière, introduced around 1939, had circular stitched cups which shaped and pointed the bust more than ever before. The ideal was not a full bust, pushed forward, as it had been around the turn of the century, but a high, firm and youthful bustline. Brassières in particular changed shape during this period.

Advertisement for Hollywood Maxwell circular stitched brassière, launched in 1939.

„HOLLYWOOD-*Maxwell*"
HIGH CLASS BRASSIERES

Still of Marlene Dietrich in daring clothing from the film *The Blue Angel*, 1930.

Women's and weekly magazines often carried advertisements featuring pictures of American film stars, who were excellent promoters of the feminine image idealized in the 1930s. They were characterized as young, attractive and elegant, but their freshness was also underlined. Joan Crawford, for example, was held up as an example both of the fresh sportswoman and of the elegant lady. A *femme fatale* like Marlene Dietrich, on the other hand, could not be used in women's magazines. Her erotic image was not in keeping with the prevalent feminine ideal. Her breakthrough came in Josef von Sternberg's film *The Blue Angel* (1930), in which her portrayal of a sexy cabaret singer made her the sophisticated sex idol of the 1930s.

The keynote of the female ideal again became femininity – displaying not the voluptuous forms and tiny, corseted waist that had been the ideal for most of the nineteenth century, but softly accentuated contours. However, as during the Victorian era, beauty was associated with traditional female virtues such as respectability, decency and compliance – all of which were important for the maintenance of middle-class moral standards, of which women again became the guardians.

The freedom that women had achieved in the post-war period could not be maintained when the economic crisis began to take hold in 1930, leading to the Depression throughout the Western world. The feminine ideal changed almost immediately from the emancipated and self-confident tomboy ideal of the 1920s to an elegant, 'ladylike' ideal. A fashion article in 1931 expressed the feeling thus:

The ladylike and stylish look, no matter how remarkable it may sound in our sports- and outdoor-loving age, is the feminine and fashion ideal of the moment. One *must* look like a Daughter of Eve and not like the modern Adam!

Women were to be feminine, decent and muted again; their appearance had to be attractive but not sensual and under no circumstances was it to be offensive or show signs of a desire for emancipation. Hairstyles were still relatively short, but now with soft waves or small curls; the cloche hat developed a brim in various sizes and the dress fell softly and gracefully around the figure. This was a feminine ideal that clearly indicated the altered position of women in society – a return to old ideals and the old pattern of gender roles.

When the Nazis came to power under Hitler's leadership in Germany in 1933 and as their cultural programme and attitude to women spread, the atmosphere of freedom and many of the democratic advances that had been made after the First World War disappeared.

The Nazis resisted all modern movements in literature and art, claiming

Summer dresses in feminine styles – all with smooth hips and fuller skirts, 1930.

that they were harmful to the German spirit and morality. A number of modern books and magazines, including a valuable collection of books from the Institute for Sex Research, were burnt as pornography. The Nazis also removed from museums all works of art that they considered to be depraved, 'un-German' or hostile – works they termed 'Entartete Kunst' – and destroyed or sold many of them abroad. The writer Elsa Gress, who went on a number of journeys to Germany in the gloom of the 1930s, gives her impression of Nazism at work in her book *Free as a Bird and Foreign*:

I clearly remember the following day: a visit to a travelling exhibition of 'entartete Kunst' which was intended to show the faithful all across the country the horrors the Nazis were freeing them from before these horrors were destroyed. The exhibition was free for young people, since they had to learn their lesson properly and we went in – it was the only exhibition we could afford on that trip and most definitely the best we could have seen anywhere in Europe for all the money in the world.[2]

Nazism's attitude to women was reactionary and repressive. Women's activities were to be limited to the three K's: 'Kinder, Küche und Kirche' (children, kitchen and church). Their social importance was reduced to that of being good wives and mothers and to bearing Aryan children. In his opening speech at the large *Die Frau (The Woman)* exhibition in Berlin, Goebbels warned women against becoming involved in politics, 'since it sullies the female soul and should, therefore, be left to men'.[3]

A good German was not allowed to smoke in public and demands for moral rectitude were intensified, especially for women. All signs of the emancipation women had achieved in the Roaring 1920s were forbidden and the old ideal of chastity was brought out and dusted off again. One sign of the importance of this decent feminine ideal for Nazi ideology was the fact that modern women's bathing costumes were forbidden. It was felt in Germany that bathing costumes had become far too provocative, if not outright indecent, so they had to find some way of eliminating the beast. The question was debated thoroughly by a special committee at the ministry. The result was an agreement with producers of bathing costumes to produce only those models that the ministry had approved.[4]

Nazism fought against any form of eroticism in the female body; it had to be discreet, decent and concealed – just as sexuality did. A more liberal attitude to sex adopted by both sexes in the 1920s had reduced prostitution. Now stricter expectations of moral rectitude encouraged the development of double standards, allowing prostitution to flourish once again. The pornography industry exploited the sexual hunger that the restrictive morality of the Depression had brought about, producing much-sought-after pictures and stories.

Fully buttoned coat dress with cape in elegant cut by Mirande, 1931.

The reactionary currents in Germany spread irresistibly to the rest of Europe, but cultural radicals tried to establish a kind of 'cultural front'. In Denmark, they formed a humanistic movement to fight against Nazism and encroachments on democracy. Poul Henningsen wrote:

Trying to understand and justify the burning of books can lead to no other conclusion than that there is Nazism in the Danish psyche. So we must expect soon a wave of moral rectitude with all its symptoms, such as the banning of bathing costumes, etc. We can see clearly what awaits us, in the form of earlier ladies' fashions such as leg-of-mutton sleeves, organdie and frills. We are returning to a time when sex cannot be discussed, and can only be done in secret and when the human body is expected to remain hidden.[5]

He pointed out that Nazism was not a geographical phenomenon, but a political/ideological one, and it could also spread to Denmark. Therefore it was important to realize the danger and to fight against its domestic manifestations. 'Twilight is well advanced in Denmark,' he wrote in his cultural–political manifesto *What about Culture?* (1933).[6] His central concept was cultural coherence: that there is a coherence between all facets of life, both spiritual and material; and that the art and the culture of a society are products of the same economic and ideological conditions. He believed that the worldwide Depression and the events in Germany were causing a swing towards conservatism in Denmark, even a Nazification of people's way of thinking; at the same time, culture, morality, aesthetics and the social position of women were also tending in the same direction.

The Depression of the 1930s brought mass unemployment. People fought for the jobs that remained. In the boom of the 1920s many women had had good jobs, and even kept them when they got married, ignoring the middle-class attitude that a woman's place was in the home. Now the lack of jobs for women on the labour market was the impetus to force self-supporting married women off the labour market and home to their 'natural' occupation as housewives and mothers. It was thought that forcing married women off the labour market and giving their jobs to men was a reasonable solution to the problem of unemployment. Women's organizations naturally protested strongly, asserting the constitutional right of women to paid employment. However, the law was one thing and practice quite another.

The struggle to remain on the labour market was the most important struggle women faced in the 1930s. Losing that fight meant social and financial misery for the large group of self-supporting married women of the working classes. But middle-class families also found it difficult to manage on one income and many women earned some extra money by, for example, taking in sewing; this was mostly done in secret so that the family's reputation would not be damaged.

The 1930s were hard for most people, but especially for women, who had to accept that many of the freedoms and equal opportunities they had won in various areas were being taken away again, partly by a witch-hunt against working women and partly by propaganda agitating for women to adhere to their true 'nature'. The freer relationship between the sexes that had been established in the 1920s now also lost ground, resulting in a clear differentiation between the sexes, evident in the male and female ideals that emerged. Again the notion that women's primary destiny was marriage came to the fore, and women were again expected to take care of the family and the home. But marriage no longer offered an assured security for women, as divorces became more and more frequent. It was, therefore, quite unrealistic to maintain that marriage was an appropriate institution for all women – not least because there were still more women than men.

Beauty was an asset, which, as we have seen, made it easier for a woman to get married and to keep her husband's interest. An attractive appearance was important in any case, or at least this is what the beauty propaganda proclaimed to its women readers. Most fashion and women's magazines had a permanent 'beauty' feature and offered various exercise and diet programmes too.

In around 1938 the Standard Pattern Company launched the new 'Slimming Corset' with woven-in ventilation holes. Great claims were made for it:

While you walk and stand the elastic rubber works with your body and with a lightly vibrating massage removes excess grammes and creates a slender, harmonious and supple figure.

Propaganda naturally increased women's self-awareness and most of them tried to live up to the ideals of beauty and slimness: it could hardly be said to encourage them to think in terms of emancipation. Few had the ideal shape naturally, but by healthy living, exercise and body care, and the right kind of corsetry, the ideal could be achieved. Having a 'healthy mind in a healthy body' cost time and money, however. Sport and exercise were eventually the only activities in which no limits were set on women's physical participation: on the contrary, it was thought that the pursuit of health and fitness would strengthen the female body and promote a healthy soul!

Everyday dresses in the 1930s became longer, more comely and ladylike. Legs were no longer in the spotlight, although they became increasingly visible in the many sports and leisure activities women took part in. Different types of women's trousers became more common; for example, shorts for cycling and holidays and beach pyjamas with long, wide legs for walking on the beach. But it was unthinkable that respectable women should wear long trousers for work or in fashionable city life.

A hopeful fashion article appeared in a women's magazine in 1930:

Rumour would have it that the fashion kings are preparing an autumn coup: trousers are coming!

Young women wear them for sport. We swear by them and would not give them up for love nor money. We wear beach pyjamas at the coast, and at intimate afternoon teas we receive our lady friends in dreamy pyjamas made of wonderful fabrics. And now it seems that trousers may be about to win their last and greatest victory and supplant our day and evening dresses. What do you think, ladies? We secretly look forward with glee to the panic, protests and violent rebellion there will be if the rumours are correct. [7]

Many years passed, however, before trousers became common as everyday wear for women. Nevertheless, the fashion designer Elsa Schiaparelli

Everyday dresses became relatively long and very respectable in the 1930s.

Bathing costumes by Patou and Vionnet, and costume with shorts and bolero by Bonwit Teller, 1931.

launched elegant party pyjamas in silk, decorated with her characteristic embroideries.

A new kind of corsetry appeared in 1935 for use under trousers: the American pantie-girdle, often produced in lastex net. Underwear consisted of a short chemise and knickers. French knickers were very popular. Cami-knickers, a combination of chemise and knickers, were also worn, but combinations remained popular. Tricot charmeuse, satin and crêpe-de-chine were the most popular fabrics for the more elegant models, and artificial silk underwear was affordable for a larger group of women. Shaped vests and knickers in knitted cotton or wool were worn for everyday use.

The opposite of the respectable, decent feminine ideal, which dominated in the period of moral rearmament of the 1930s, was the 'dangerous' woman with sex appeal, usually positioned outside the norms of family life. But towards the end of 1939 a different type emerged – more curvaceous, with the breasts and waist accentuated by corsetry. Again, protests were provoked, this time under the guise of concern for women's health, as for example in this newspaper article of November 1939:

There is no hiding the fact – indeed, fashion underlines it – that the wasp waist is on its way back. For a time we had the slender, boyish look. This was replaced by a more feminine ideal, and women could once again be proud of the fact that

Edward Steichen's photograph for the front cover of *Vogue*, July 1932, epitomizes the 1930s feminine body aesthetic: healthy, slender, supple and suntanned.

they had hips and a bust. This feminine look has become more and more pronounced: the bust has been lifted, full skirts have become fashionable, bustle-like draping around the hips has appeared and now the new winter fashions are nearly all suggesting the wasp waist. It is part of the new line. . . .

But modern women do not want to be laced up. The new figure is not in tune with the way of life of modern, sporty women. . . . Large demonstrations against the corset . . . have taken place in the United States.

And the following editorial appeared in the American magazine *Corset and Underwear* in September 1939:

Mrs Adam Gimbel, wife of the president of Saks–Fifth Avenue, upon her return from Paris, said: 'Small waists and new corsets are coming back. American women are going to be more luxurious. Clothes are to be very elaborate with heavy brocades and small waists and the new corsets are going to be the fashion. They are very beautiful but uncomfortable, but women will wear them. Women will wear anything if it's fashion. We have had comfort for years, now we are going to be dignified. You have to hold your head up with a corset. Everybody has to be dignified wearing corsets.'

Under normal circumstances, the debate about corsets would probably have continued until the fashion had been accepted, as had so often happened before, but the Second World War halted the development of this fashion and therefore of the debate.

Clothes rationing was introduced in Britain in 1941 and a combination of recycling and ingenuity became necessary. Fabrics for use in corsets were in short supply and, in order to keep up with the demand, manufacturers started to produce them in paper. The coveted paper corsets were of remarkably good quality but unfortunately not washable!

Elsa Schiaparelli party wear, 1930s: long trousers with wide legs and short embroidered jacket.

1942 version of the 'slip-on' girdle. During the war it was produced in fabric substitute.

1945 suit by Nicholl Clothes, London: short skirt and jacket in masculine cut with broad shoulders and lapels.

Women's labour was again required during the war and women took over many jobs formerly done by men. Obviously they needed more practical clothes. Women had been wearing trousers for sport and leisure for some time; now it became acceptable to wear them for work, too.

As women took over more areas of responsibility outside the home, their clothes became more masculine. The muted, softly rounded feminine ideal of the 1930s was replaced during the war with a more self-confident and active type of woman whose body language expressed an altered self-awareness. Dresses now had wide, padded shoulders and skirts were shortened to just below the knee. The style was still slender in the hips but the clothes had a stiffer, more masculine cut and no longer embraced the body. Alongside this, there existed a more glamorous image, with curves that were accentuated, although not directly put across as attributes of sex. This ideal did not really contradict the prevalent norms and there seemed to be a need for it during the war. It was this that was the basis for the figure launched in 1947 as the 'New Look'.

8 Clearly Defined Female Forms
c. 1947–64

Many of the old Parisian fashion houses closed down during the Second World War, but after the war new ones appeared, including that of Christian Dior. In 1947 he created the look that marked his breakthrough as a fashion designer – the famous New Look. It also ushered in a golden age for French haute couture that lasted until the mid-1960s.

Dior wanted to return to elegant femininity, a welcome trend after the clothes rationing, poverty and rather masculine lifestyle and image to which women had been subjected during the war years. His New Look creations had longer, fuller skirts, the waist was small and the shape of the bust was lifted and accentuated, giving the modern hourglass figure – and this meant palmy days for the corset industry.

Dior's style was enthusiastically received all over the Western world, but it was also criticized in many quarters, partly on the grounds that the long, full dresses required metres of fabric at a time when there were still shortages in many countries; and partly on the grounds that the New Look promoted an old-fashioned ideal – of the female corseted into inactivity – and was thus reactionary and nostalgic. But, as usual, fashion won and the protests gradually died down. In the course of 1948 the fashion caught on all over Western Europe and it became the dream of many women to be able to put on one of these super-feminine creations in the new length – no more than 32cm above the ground.

A women's magazine fashion writer who had been to a showing of Dior's latest collection wrote a report that removed any uncertainty about skirt lengths:

No doubt people will go on discussing its merits and demerits, but we can rest assured that the new skirt length is already a fact – and we may just as well admit that there is not a single one of us who – whatever we said or thought before – would have a new afternoon or evening dress made in the old length. And that is all there is to it.[1]

The 'New Look' introduced by Dior in 1947: a tailored jacket in heavy silk and a full, black skirt in the new length.

The feminine ideal altered during this period, to the extent that the 1950s celebrated the slender, youthful woman, while the 1960s witnessed the beginning of the cult of extreme youth. The ideal figure remained more or less unchanged, however, with its accentuation of the breasts and waist.

Along with the fashions, artificial mannequins also acquired a new body shape to match the fashion ideal. Hindsgaul mannequins really took off in the world market in 1947; they were elegant and stylish with the accentuated bust and small waist that were then in vogue. Manufacturers tried to make the figures more mobile and lifelike, but they were still idealized and did not precisely represent natural anatomy. The mannequins were a little taller than the average woman, the legs were exaggeratedly long, the waist was smaller and the bust was higher. Thus the female physical features that were the basis of the new fashion were writ larger on the mannequins, with a view to showing off the new styles to the best advantage. The mannequins' make-up and hairstyles also helped to create the ideal fashion type. Hindsgaul's figures had either removable wigs made of horsehair or a hairstyle of the increasingly popular realistic type in which laces were inserted *(opposite far left)* Smart Danish mannequin by Hindsgaul with 'wasp waist', 1948.

(opposite left) Fashionable ideal body by Hindsgaul, 1948.

(right) This teenage mannequin was one of the first designed by Christel for Hindsgaul in 1958.

into the figure's scalp and individually styled and then treated with colours and hairsprays.

The materials and production of mannequins underwent constant development between 1947 and 1965. In 1947 they were made from a mixture of plaster and hessian; they weighed around 25kg and were very porous. Papier-mâché was then used, which was light, but difficult to make look realistic. In 1956 Hindsgaul became the first company in the world to develop a fibreglass mannequin, which fulfilled all the requirements of an artificial figure. The removable wigs were made of American nylon hair and were of various shades and thicknesses. The new 'Rytmica' models, which came on the market in 1964, were articulated in nearly all their joints. They now weighed only 7kg, whereas the old wax mannequins had weighed around 50kg.

The term 'teenager' appeared at the beginning of the 1950s and the fashion industry increasingly tuned in to the buying power of these young consumers. Both teenage and adult mannequins were produced, but the differences between them dwindled to the point where, from about 1960, it was really only the hairstyle that gave any indication of

The new 'Rytmica' mannequin by Hindsgaul, 1964. Almost every joint was articulated.

age. The figures were slender and girlish, with firm, high breasts, a small waist, narrow hips and long legs. The dummies had the potential to appear quite lifelike but they were often put clumsily in artificial poses, with arms and fingers sticking out at unnatural angles, so that they ended up looking like dolls.

The female body did show off its sexual attributes, but in a strange, affected way, without any kind of sensuality. In this, it shared something with the feminine ideal of the Victorian period, which combined sexual definition with self-control, attractiveness with modesty. Even though women in the 1950s and 1960s had achieved a higher degree of freedom and social equality than ever before, a puritanical attitude to sex lingered on, forcing women to assume a certain degree of passivity if they wanted to be considered respectable.

There were differences between the feminine ideals of 1947 and 1964, but the body image of the period still reflected a view of women as sex objects. Various items of corsetry were displayed exclusively on busts designed especially for certain types of corset and brassière. They were made of plaster and hessian, glass fibre or plexiglass, in matt grey and black.

It was principally the breasts and waist that were accentuated in the new fashion line; the hips still had to be narrow, although the tightening of the waist gave them an added roundness. The basis for fashionable dress was, as previously, corsetry, but the ideal was glamour, not naturalness. The

The Waspie by Warner, 1947: boned, front lacing with hook-and-eye fastening at the back.

shape of a woman's body was suggested through a series of artifices. The beauty propagandists claimed that it was the duty of every woman to make herself beautiful and attractive – a goal made more attainable by the introduction in the 1950s of many labour-saving and labour-serving devices which made housework much easier.

The new fashion shape of 1947 had a very small waist, which required much greater figure control around the waist. It became fashionable to wear boned belt corsets in an hourglass shape, laced at the back and with hooks and eyes at the front or the side. They were made of brocade, silk or

cotton satin and were salmon-coloured or pink, still the dominant colours until 1950. A boned 'waspie', which could be worn over the girdle or roll-on, was also very popular. The fashion for very tight corsets lasted for only a short time: modern women did not readily accept having their freedom of movement limited.

From the beginning of the 1950s, many models of corset and girdle had a high waist, which, with the help of darts or spiral boning, created a slender waist. They were often made of elastic net, which consisted of nylon power net or lastex, with silk lastex at the sides and for the gussets. Many of the models had fixed front panels of nylon with satin crossbands which slimmed and smoothed any superfluous padding. They were fastened with hooks and eyes or zips at the side. White and black were the favourite colours, although salmon pink was still used for full corsets with greater support, often made of cotton-drill, brocade or satin.

Roll-ons and roll-on panties were a lighter form of corsetry, mainly worn by younger women. They were made of nylon elastic net or another type of elastic fabric which could be rolled on and gave the waist a natural appearance. Nylon thread had been invented in 1930 in the American DuPont chemical laboratories by Dr W. Hill, but it was not until 1939

Net elastic girdle with 'ribbons' front panel by Treo, 1956.

that nylon stockings were ready for the market – as a trial. One year later, sixty million pairs of nylon stockings had been sold to American women. The production of nylon stockings was well underway when the Japanese attacked Pearl Harbor on 7 December 1941 and brought the United States into the Second World War. All connections with Japan and the Japanese silk industry ceased and in any case nylon was needed for more important things than stockings. The mass production of nylon stockings really got underway after the war; they were initially expensive to buy, but out-competed silk stockings relatively quickly. From the customer's point of view, the semi-transparent nylon and its related fabric perlon were easy to wash, dried quickly and needed no ironing.

Nylon underwear really caught on in the 1950s, its cheapness helping to democratize clothing. Never before had so many women had the opportunity to wear elegant underwear. For everyday use tailored nylon or perlon slips with a shaped bust, pleats and nylon lace were worn with simple knickers. Under evening dresses, fluffy ballerina skirts of paper nylon with several layers of tulle were worn, invoking associations with the earlier crinoline period.

The modern corseted figure with the full, raised bust was very much the vogue in the 1950s, although the ideal shape of the bust underwent several changes, each time attracting public debate on this delicate matter.

In 1947 most brassières were still made of satin or brocade, but nylon was the most common fabric from the beginning of the 1950s, and throughout the period Hollywood Maxwell was the leading brand of brassière. Their sophisticated designs and good fit in all models made them the most popular brassières in the United States. In 1958, Hollywood Maxwell changed its name to Hollywood Vassarette, thought to be a better brand name for the American market, and production expanded to include other types of corsetry. Many different types of brassière were produced. One of the best-selling types, and the one that perhaps epitomized the era, was made of nylon and had nylon lace in the bust. It had circular stitched cups, which gave the breasts the desired ample and pointed shape (the 'torpedo' shape), and was underwired.

Underwiring began to be used around 1954 when Dior launched his new high bustline. This required the bust to be 6cm higher than previously, which meant that the distance from the middle of the breast to the shoulder should be no more than 19cm. This new idea raised a storm, the position and size of women's breasts becoming the hot topic of the autumn: panicked consumers sent telegrams to the newspapers and the issue was debated as vehemently as if a new world war were about to break out. These were great days for the kings of fashion in Paris, who still had unlimited power to dictate the body's lines and therefore the position of the bust too. Dior called his new fashion the H-line, which started a rumour that the female figure was on its way back to the straight, flat-chested, tomboy shape of the 1920s. One manager of a dress department tried to calm things down:

'There is no need for all the fuss,' he said. 'Where the idea of the ironing-board has come from I have no idea, but it is very wide of the mark. That is quite simply not Dior's style.

'Now that he has created all this fuss, and made himself unpopular with everyone from Marilyn Monroe to brassière producers, it is quite interesting to be able to say something about his collection as it really is and as it has been seen by fashion people who have been to the latest shows.

'The bust is neither to be flattened nor to disappear! It just has to be lifted a little, and to be pushed in slightly from below – and as a result of that little trick, we get the most feminine bust line since the Rococo.'[2]

No one was allowed to know before the launch how the corset that was to provide the basis for Dior's H-line was to be constructed. 'It is being guarded just as jealously as the hydrogen bomb,' said one of the fashion king's assistants in awed tones.[3]

Naturally this statement only caused even more excitement. Everyone taking part in the half-yearly show, from the fashion designers to fashion

Brassière by Hollywood Maxwell with three-quarter cups and halterneck strap..

journalists, helped to build up the atmosphere of sensation – with just a little seriousness mixed in, as the occasion deserved.

The secret behind Dior's H-line proved to be a tight lastex corset which modelled the figure from just under the bust and down across the hips. It had lace half-cups which supported and lifted the bust higher and created a new silhouette. Dior's new fashion line was not just a whim; what he especially wanted was to get away from the ideal of the exceptionally full bust, which he believed had become the object of vulgar attention, not least because of the current rivalry between over-endowed sex bombs. Dior launched the high 'Rococo bosom' and narrow hips, but there were other fashion houses in Paris that promoted a more curvy look; Geneviève Fath's designs, for example, strongly accentuated the waist and the rounding of the hips and made the bust fuller and not quite as high as Dior did. Her line nevertheless also required a good corset or corselette as a foundation.

The brassière also changed shape. Of most interest were the new models of brassière from Hollywood Maxwell which were a modified form of Dior's line. The new models had three-quarter cups with inset foam pads and underwiring which supported and lifted the bust into a more voluptuous curve than full cups did.

The popular pointed brassière with circular stitched cups by Hollywood Maxwell, produced in three different models.

Stars from Hollywood

Hollywood Maxwell

For wear under the décolleté evening dresses that were then fashionable, Hollywood Maxwell presented bras with several new designs of shoulder strap. The new 'three-quarter-time' shape, as it was called, had shoulder straps far out at the sides both in the conventional and in the new halter-neck model. A strapless model was also made. This new shaping miracle from Hollywood Maxwell was written about widely in the press and was in all the window displays.

White and black were the dominant colours in corsetry in the 1950s; salmon pink became less common. Warner Brothers introduced different

Advertisement for Warner's 'Alphabet' brassières, produced in four cup sizes, A–D.

cup sizes in 1935, but it was not until the end of the 1940s that the four cup sizes A,B,C and D became common.

The pointed brassière, called the 'sweater girl bra', reached its greatest popularity in 1957, after which the bust line became less tight and full. The fashionable dress in the sack or chemise shape now fell loosely, or, as in the trapeze line that followed in 1958, skimmed the figure. The trapeze line was the creation of the young Yves Saint-Laurent, presenting his first collection for the Dior fashion house after Dior's death the previous year. Nevertheless, women still wore corsets to enhance their shape. The various loose-fitting fashions of the late 1950s were not intended to re-create the tomboy ideal of the 1920s; nor was any message of emancipation connected with them. The ideal was feminine, but the forms that expressed it were voluptuous, near caricatures of femininity.

Marilyn Monroe, Jayne Mansfield and Diana Dors, the sex idols of the 1950s, all flaunted their feminine attributes. Other women were not so well endowed. Fortunately, there was help to be had for this 'deficiency'. Some brassières were made with foam padding; others had specially sewn pockets for extra padding. Loose, pointed foam pads were also available. Some women, and especially young girls, stuffed their brassières with cotton wool or other padding. The disadvantage of these 'false' breasts was that they were inclined to lose their shape if they were pushed or touched, which could be very embarrassing.

The film stars had their own secret – the 'Bleumette', a kind of 'invisible' bra to improve the appearance of the bust, made by a top New York designer. It consisted of two separate cups, which were stuck on under the breasts to lift them up. They cost $2.98 per pair and could be used once only, which rather limited their popularity. But, as the advertisement said, the 'miracle bra' was 'just made for glamorous occasions'.

The bra was an obligatory item of clothing to suit the feminine ideal of the 1950s, equally essential for naturally big-busted women and for foam-rubber Venuses. Even the modern cotton lastex, silk lastex or nylon bathing suits had a built-in brassière and boning to form and accentuate the bust.

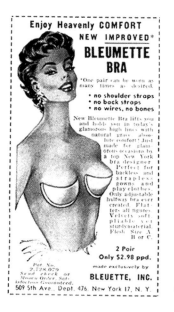

The American glamour 'Bleumette Bra', 1958.

The voluptuous Marilyn Monroe with her husband, Arthur Miller, photographed in 1957.

One commentator on the history of dress wrote in 1953 of the modern brassière's harmful effects:

The brassière is gaining so much in popularity as to render civilised women incapable of breastfeeding. No gland can take prolonged pressure. The breast glands are now permanently bandaged. This strapping also inhibits the connective tissue that should bear the weight of the breast.[4]

This criticism sparked a debate in the press about how tight a brassière should be and how much it could lift and support without damaging the breasts. In a follow-up article, the above writer cautioned that the bust was not suited to being hung up in straps, but recognised that the brassière had 'a masochistic function. The wearer likes the feeling of constriction',[5] and that women wore brassières to accentuate the bust and thus to assert themselves:

The foolish belief in all male-dominated, patriarchal cultures that the male sex is by nature superior to women because the man has the organ of reproduction has to be countered by the fact that men cannot give birth. Women demonstrate this by showing off their bust. The only problem is that it is often an empty demonstration.[6]

The attack on the tight brassière was probably justifiable on the grounds of health, but it is hard to take the writer's 'explanation' of the fashion for brassières seriously. He trotted out one pseudo-scientific explanation after another for the fashion, knowing perfectly well that fashion has never taken account of the wearer's health. The tight, flat brassière of the 1920s was no less harmful than the tight, pointed brassière of the 1950s, but provoked no protests because the tomboy figure and loose dresses of the 1920s were associated by many with an emancipated feminine ideal.

Audrey Hepburn's slender girlish body in black jersey and ballerina shoes made her the idol of teenage girls in the 1950s.

Anita Ekberg demonstrates her feminine advantages. Still from Federico Fellini's film *La Dolce Vita*, 1959.

'The Merry Widow', Warner's elegant torsolette in black or white nylon, was named after a 1952 film of the same name in which Lana Turner wore a stiffened corselette.

Of course most men found this focus on the bust wonderful, more so than did women. Sexual morality for women was still restrictive. Young girls were supposed to require a lot of coaxing before they gave in and men would thus regard them as 'nice' girls – and if they did give in, other people would label them as less nice and warn them that they risked 'going off the rails'. Big-breasted sex idols such as Marilyn Monroe, Sophia Loren, Gina Lollobrigida and Anita Ekberg were more a fulfilment of men's dreams than an expression of female self-confidence. Many young girls especially would rather have looked like the slender, girlish Audrey Hepburn, who radiated a youthful freshness and sweetness.

Fashion's demand that women have the 'perfect' figure and the 'right' forms had at the time something of the nature of compulsion about it.

The pointed breasts, the constricted waist and the high stiletto heels, which caused a slightly rocking gait, were all artificial devices that accentuated a view of women as sex objects.

In 1954 a new article of underwear became available. Shorter than the corselet and strapless, the torsolette, as it was called, was intended to control the female torso from the breasts down to the waist in one piece. It was mostly made of nylon or nylon lace with elastic in the sides and back. It had three-quarter cups with underwiring and foam padding and was fastened with hooks and eyes at the front or at the back.

In 1958, a new elastic material called Lycra was invented and developed by DuPont in the USA, the same company that had invented nylon. Lycra was an epoch-making innovation for the corset industry and meant lighter, softer and longer-lasting elasticated products, which had greater potential for figure control. Lycra has been a major element in a great deal of corsetry and sportswear up to the present day.

The style of the 1950s was elegant and very feminine, almost as if created to confirm the myth of women as the 'fair sex'. The fashions were dictated from Paris and French fashions in women's clothes reigned supreme; but at the same time a new generation of consumers had grown up who required more things from clothes than Parisian high fashion provided. In the boom years after the war many young people were paid more and had more free time than young people had had before. This phenomenon, along with changed attitudes to and among the young, created a need for an independent means of expression. The fashion industry wasted no time in exploiting the commercial potential of increased consumption.

Previously, department stores had had separate departments for girls' and boys' clothes, from the age of three to about thirteen or fourteen. After that, children became adults and had to accept adult norms for clothes. Now, for the first time in history, clothes were designed especially for the age group between childhood and adulthood. From 1950 onwards teenage departments were established and teenage fashion shows were held. The shows were very popular and the clothes shown were quite different from adult clothes: smart and girlish, much influenced by American 'college fashion', and looking as if they had been cut out of *Seventeen*, an American fashion magazine for young girls. The teenage mannequins were also fresh and natural types.

However, a natural shape was out, even for young girls. As soon as their breasts began to develop, they would be encased in what was effectively a straitjacket. A brassière was obligatory for girls by the time they turned fourteen. To keep up the demand, the corset manufacturers had to come up with a rationale. They could not say, as they did in promoting their products to adult women, that the 'right' brassière would give the wearer a

Hollywood Maxwell's teenage brassière with quilted cups, 1956.

Teenage clothes, 1956: summer dresses with stiffened skirts and jeans.

firm, youthful bust. Young girls already had that. Instead, they produced teen bras for busts that were on the fuller side – and padded models for girls who thought they were inadequately endowed, as of course many did, given the dictates of the industry.

At the end of the 1950s, coloured corsetry began to be produced for the youngsters, but until 1960, 85 per cent of the underwear sold to adults and young women was white, 10 per cent was black and only 5 per cent was coloured. At the beginning of the 1960s Hollywood Vassarette created a range of patterned underwear for teenagers, consisting of brassières, girdles, roll-ons and panties in several colour combinations, made of nylon lace and Lycra lace net.

The 'teenage' concept marked a distinct break with the attitudes and styles of adults, but it did not consist of just one fashion or style for all teenagers. The concept included various modes of expression, both social and sexual.

'College style', which was very popular with well brought-up young girls of the 1950s, came from America. So did the confrontational style of the 'leather jackets', which was a means by which some young men could visibly demonstrate their wish to rebel against the false 'niceness' of middle-class ideals. Films such as *The Wild One* (1953) with the leather-clad Marlon Brando in the lead role, and *Rebel Without a Cause* (1955), starring James Dean, which had its première two weeks after his tragic death,

Pleasing suit designed by Fath, 1955 – as a contrast to the leather jackets on a poster for the film *On the Waterfront*.

introduced a new kind of youth idol who, together with rock stars, became the objects of hero worship for young girls and boys.

The various youth subcultures that arose in the 1950s deliberately distanced themselves from the older generation in their preferences for clothes, music and leisure interests, but sex roles were structured along the same patriarchal lines, which meant that there was a significant difference between female and male modes of expression. The boys drew attention to themselves: they were rebellious, provocative, sometimes violent in their response to what they saw as class and generational conflicts. Moreover, all the youth idols were men. By contrast, girls were almost invisible in those subcultures: their behaviour and dress conformed with the norms, although they did create certain independent modes of expression which signalled both their acceptance of the prevailing feminine ideal and their membership of a particular class.

Working-class girls tended to leave school earlier than middle- and upper-class girls and and were thus exposed much sooner to the demands to be attractive and thus ultimately marriageable. Looking attractive was a boon in other areas too: for example, it offered a short cut to a career in the movies, giving girls from more humble backgrounds the opportunity to achieve a higher social status than their education would otherwise have given them.

172

The very curvaceous feminine ideal of the 1950s, which became popular with Dior's 'New Look' in 1947, was not merely a reaction to the shortages and the rather masculine image of the war: as early as 1939 there had been a trend towards accentuating female forms. The feminine ideal fitted in very well with the post-war consolidation of middle-class family ideology, which positioned woman as the central figure in the nuclear family. As the situation after the war reached normality again, people fell back into their traditional gender roles, despite the fact that more women than ever before were studying or pursuing vocational qualifications. This was mainly a safety measure in case they did not get married or the marriage did not last – the number of broken marriages was increasing. Women usually studied for a shorter time than men of the same social class, since their prime object was still to get married and have children.

A great deal of propaganda was put out in the 1950s to keep intact the feminine ideal of the post-war boom years: the woman who could manage a household, make sure that her family thrived and at the same time stay looking young and attractive, as it was her duty to do. Housework had become easier with the invention of many labour-saving devices, especially kitchen appliances; modern child-rearing, on the other hand,

This advertisement from Asani is typical of the 1950s. Women were constantly being reminded to be well-presented and attractive.

made more demands on mothers, who were required to be more sensitive to their children's individual needs and development. I believe that many women put aside their own desires and needs in order to take care of their families, because the inhumanity of the war had fostered a longing for security in everyone. A large number of women gave up their jobs and careers in order to devote themselves wholeheartedly to being 'real' women: good housekeepers, loving mothers and attractive wives. Simone de Beauvoir believed that the latter was a trap:

In order to realize her femininity a woman is required to make herself into both object and prey, that is, she must renounce her claims to be a sovereign subject. It is this conflict that marks the situation of the emancipated woman especially ... To renounce her femininity is to renounce a part of her humanity. Misogynist men have often reproached intellectual women for 'neglecting themselves'; but at the same time they have told them, 'If you wish to be our equals, stop using make-up and nail-polish.' This is nonsense. It is precisely because the concept of femininity is artificially shaped by custom and fashion that it is imposed upon each woman from without ... Nothing fundamental is changed thereby: the individual is still not free to do as she pleases. The woman who does not conform to the concept of femininity devalues herself sexually and hence socially, since sexual values are an integral feature of society.[7]

De Beauvoir believed that if women continued to be fully and wholly feminine, it was because they wanted to give themselves the greatest possible chances of success with the opposite sex. Breaking the conventions, breaking the balance of power that makes women into 'Women', is a rebellion, with consequences that women have to be prepared to accept.

Very few women in the 1950s were prepared to take up the struggle against this kind of sex discrimination. Most women tried to live up to the beauty ideal, because by doing so they met the requirements for femininity, but this also kept them in the role of the 'fair sex' and meant that they had to fight to be taken seriously in other contexts. But the dilemma of women has always been the myth of femininity, producing in many a somewhat ambivalent attitude to their own sex and its outward manifestations.

Marilyn Monroe was the most celebrated star in the Hollywood of the 1950s and probably the one woman who most obviously suffered at the hands of the female myth. She had a very special aura of childlike innocence and womanly sweetness; she was sensitive and vulnerable and yearned to be accepted as a human being and an actress, not just as a sex object. In the end, she could not take the demands and limitations of the female myth and took her own life.

Many other women felt similarly constrained by the merciless requirement to be attractive. If they had had the choice of making themselves

Marilyn Monroe, 1956.

beautiful because it was both a pleasure and self-affirming, or of ignoring the issue without being degraded as sexual beings by men, then female beauty would not have been used to quite the same extent in the power struggle between the sexes. Barbara Sichtermann writes:

When women beautify themselves, it is largely to adjust to the prevailing ideal, and it is the nature of that ideal, above all, that determines whether the adjustment is considered as playful or a repressive limitation of female individuality.[8]

Brigitte Bardot, 1958.

The demand that all women be beautiful is itself utopian but, as Sichter-mann points out, the nature of the changing feminine ideal decides how far that demand is met.

In the 1950s, female forms were accentuated as sexual attributes, but the physical ideal did not classify women socially as it had done in the past when elegant, tasteful dress was an expression of the excess of time and money of the privileged class. Nevertheless, conformity with the correct attire was of supreme importance.

'Beauty, harmony and correctness are the three cornerstones of dress, and one should try to live up to these three requirements,' was the precept offered in *Femina* in 1957, when the magazine launched its 'Become a new woman' campaign:

Become a new woman, not just on the outside, but also on the inside. Let us give renewed inspiration to the women of the mid-twentieth century . . . the century that has to a great degree belonged to women.

Some women may protest that there is too much talk about clothes, beauty care and so on . . . but it must not be forgotten that a woman's appearance is one of her most important assets in her struggle to exist, whether she works inside or outside the home.

It is hard to see where the renewal was. There had in fact been no change of any note in adult women's clothing since Dior had launched the New Look a decade previously. The 'new woman' campaign did not change the prevailing norms for dress, either. The only impact it had was to establish a more youthful ideal. It was not only adult women's clothes that changed and became less 'ladylike'; there was also a significant change in teenage clothes, which until then had borne the mark of American college style. Young girls' clothes became more sex-determined; there was a kind of reciprocal action between the two age groups, which meant that the borders between teenage and adult clothes became more fluid.

Dresses had slowly become shorter, but full skirts were still favourites, especially among the very young who enthusiastically starched their frilly cotton underskirts, or had a curtain wire sewn into the hem so that they stuck out stiffly. The full skirt gained even more in popularity after the French film star Brigitte Bardot got married in 1958 wearing a checked cotton dress with a full skirt in little-girl style. Launched in the film *And God Created Woman* (1956), with sensual shape, slightly childish pout and long tousled hair, Bardot represented a new style. Though more liberated and untraditional in her behaviour and clothes, she was no less feminine or sexy than the 'adult' sex idols of the day. Her talent was mainly physical.

Gradually, many young girls took over the tight skirt of adult women's dress, which they wore with a blouse or twinset and pointed stilettos. Just like their mothers, young girls were exposed to the beauty ideal, from a very early age, and defined themselves in relation to the ideal, not totally rigidly but in a way that expressed their varying lifestyles and self-awareness and was conditioned by the class to which they belonged.

Not until the beginning of the 1960s did young girls begin to break with the prevailing demands for femininity, marking their protest against being kept as passive sex objects in new physical modes of expression.

Mini dresses with 'op-art' patterns by Pierre Cardin, 1966.

9 Physical Desexualization
c. 1965–78

A very youthful feminine ideal caught on in 1965: the new fashion ideal was a thin, little-girl type without any obvious female characteristics, similar to the lanky, tomboy fashion of the 1920s, which had also tried to eliminate feminine contours so as to free women from the confines of the role of sex object. Young women rebelled against the perpetuation of the ideal of overblown femininity, which they believed contributed to sex discrimination, and instead cultivated a desexualized, pubescent ideal.

The British designer Mary Quant played a decisive role in creating a revolution in fashion – not just in clothes but in a whole new mode of physical expression. She started her career at the end of the 1950s by producing original, fun clothes for young people at her little shop in Chelsea in London. Her style, which threw out all previous notions of correctness in clothing, was received enthusiastically by young people as a sign of their departure from tradition. Paris had hitherto dictated fashion but now its dominance had been broken and the 'Swinging London' of the 1960s set the agenda in music and fashion for young people.

Mary Quant designed clothes for ordinary people – clothes that could be mass-produced for a youth market – but her real breakthrough came in 1965 when she launched her miniskirt. Another version was shown at the same time by André Courrèges in Paris, where it caused a sensation. Quite soon the mini, originally aimed at the very young, was also being worn by a lot of adult women. Both Mary Quant and Courrèges contributed to the breaking down of age barriers in dress and of other conventions. They also introduced a new form of fashion show at which the models no longer paraded sedately down the catwalk but danced to beat music.

The cult of youth brought with it a change of fashion ideal. The miniskirt was produced in many shapes and sizes by young fashion designers, but its straight lines, which accentuated neither waist nor hips, were a constant in the design. The fashionable female body was turned into a set of geometrical shapes, a trend seen also in the decoration of the clothes, such as 'op-art' patterns or 'pop-art' pictures borrowed from painting. Op-art was clearly inspired by the non-figurative, straight-lined, clear-coloured

Simple mini dress and white boots by Courrèges, 1965.

'Pop-art' creations by Yves Saint-Laurent, 1966.

or black-and-white compositions of Mondrian. In 1965 Yves Saint-Laurent designed a collection called 'Mondrian', inspired by the artist's paintings from the 1920s. Pop-art was a more recent movement which tried to break through the barriers of 'high' art. One of the main figures was the multimedia artist Andy Warhol, whose unconventional images were used as decoration for clothes to signal something quite other than 'good taste' and status.

In general, young people distanced themselves more and more from current morality and from the consumerism that continued unhindered in the prosperity of the 1960s. The revolt broke out in full force in 1968, when young people took to the streets to show their anger against materialism and imperialism. The uprisings did not lead to social breakdown, but they left their mark, not least because some members of the youth 'anti-culture' created alternative lifestyles in rejection of middle-class society and its conventions.

Although women now had greater independence, better qualifications and far wider employment opportunities than their predecessors, the

Twiggy in a design by Mary Quant, 1966.

little-girl ideal of the 1960s endured, expressing the protest of women against their relegation to inferior roles in society and their treatment as sex objects. The fashion was for women to look thin and girlish for as long as their weight and development could be kept under control. Many girls started on dangerous diets in order to look like the British model Twiggy, whose boyish, almost flat body became the dominating fashion ideal of the late 1960s. She was not, primarily, presented as sexually attractive and was therefore an appropriate icon for the women's liberation movement, which started in 1970.

The women's lib movement was not a unique phenomenon, but was one of many 'anti' movements which arose in the wake of the youth rebellion of 1968. Women's libbers, as its adherents were called, were mainly young, well-educated, middle-class women who organized a common attack on the traditional view of women and demanded genuine equality in the family and on the labour market. They rejected the ideals of femininity found among men and in women's magazines of women as wives and mothers.

Thin, youthful mannequins were in demand from the mid-1960s. Window display of 1967, inspired by the psychedelic style of the period.

Women's libbers challenged the dictatorship of fashion, which they claimed exploited women by promoting ideals for commercial gain without regard for the health or physical nature of women. Women's libbers wanted to be the equal of men, not to compete with other women for men's approval. They wanted clothes to be desexualized and all trace of their potential for seduction removed. Make-up was also out. As for the body, nothing less than total emancipation was acceptable: nothing was to be hidden or 'improved'. Women were not truly liberated until they could accept their bodies as they were. This attitude was not shared by all women, but it influenced the ideal images created in the 1970s, all of which were based on a 'natural' body form.

Mannequins, as we have noted, reflect a prevailing feminine ideal. At the beginning of the 1960s they were youthful but still obviously feminine. They had straight, backcombed nylon hair, heavy mascara and a slightly childish but sensual mouth with light-coloured lips. Their features were often those of Jean Shrimpton, then one of the most famous photo models, or of Jacqueline Kennedy. Such was the adulation of the young American First Lady that in 1962 fibreglass mannequins in her image were sold in thirty-three countries, although not in the USA.

From 1965 most female mannequins represented very young and thin pubescent girls that looked like Barbie dolls with their stereotypical, inexpressive faces surrounded by long, fair hair. The figures were often placed as if in motion, with their arms and legs sticking out unnaturally to the side, to create an image of youthful energy. The British designer Adel Rootstein created a successful series of Twiggy look-alike mannequins in 1966; with thirty years' hindsight, they now look like starved teenagers.

Under the impact of the women's movement, the slim, youthful but above all natural type gained currency. Breasts were allowed their natural shape and no bra was thought necessary for support. The models were taller, slimmer and longer-legged than most women, but the representation of the body was anatomically correct and modelled to look more lifelike and expressive than previously.

The ideal of the 1970s was a self-confident woman, active but in control of herself. The figures had perfect make-up and removable wigs of artificial hair. They represented a somewhat older woman liberated from outmoded roles and expectations. Liberation of the body had also been of great importance to the early women's movement. Now, women had been released from the tight corset, but still felt obliged to use other forms of figure control in order to live up to the prevalent ideal of beauty. Many young women had become tired of this body-fixated sex role, which they regarded as a barrier to real equality between the sexes, and in response to this mood, the mini had arrived on the scene.

The feminine ideal of 1972.
Beautiful, long-limbed 'Gazelle'
mannequins designed by Christel

Matching patterned underwear series
by Triumph, 1967.

Hans Henrik Lerfeldt's erotic picture
of a woman in stockings and suspender
belt.

184

The short skirt or dress, which fell loosely about the figure, shifted attention from the body to the legs. It made tights – a combination of stockings and panties – necessary and made the roll-on and the girdle as superfluous as suspenders. Of course, the corset industry tried to maintain its commercial position by stressing the need for figure control, but increasingly it was fighting a losing battle against the idea that underwear should be comfortable and nearly invisible.

In the 1960s nearly all women wore a brassière, most of which were made of nylon or nylon lace with sides, back and shoulder straps in Lycra elastic. They were underwired, often with circular stitching in the whole cup, while the three-quarter cups had foam supports. White was still the favourite colour, but black and various coloured patterns were also worn. There was a tendency towards a more natural bustline from the mid-1960s. One novelty on the market was a transparent, flesh-coloured nylon brassière without boning or underwiring, designed by the Austro-American fashion designer Rudi Gernreich, who called it the 'No-Bra'.

Tights were worn by a lot of women. They were practical and warm in the winter, and they also conformed with the desexualization of the female body: the bare area of naked flesh above the top of the stockings, which had so stimulated men's erotic imaginations, was now a thing of the past.

Many different models of girdles and roll-ons were still being produced. The favourite material was Lycra elastic net, which was soft, supple and produced a slimming effect. But as trousers became more acceptable for women, panties became more popular. These too were mostly made of Lycra elastic net and came in different lengths of leg. Many models were tailored at the back to give the bottom a naturally rounded shape.

The women's movement attempted to abolish any form of figure-controlling underwear, claiming it contributed to the 'oppression' of women. One of the first contemporary public demonstrations against the objectivization of women and the production of beauty ideals took place in Atlantic City in 1968, where the Miss America beauty contest was being held. A group of protesters crowned a sheep as the symbolic winner and then filled a large dustbin with feminine articles such as curlers, wigs, false eyelashes, girdles and bras. The media called the event 'bra-burning' – though on this and other occasions burning probably never actually happened – and the term 'bra-burner' became synonymous not just with 'feminist' but with 'man hater'.[1]

The women's movement despised all artificial aids to beautification. At this time many women, whether in the movement or not, got rid of their bras – some for a short period, others for ever; some because they sympathized with the struggle for the liberation of women, others simply

because it became fashionable. As early as 1968 Yves Saint-Laurent had shown transparent blouses worn without a bra at his fashion show in Paris.

The first skirmishes in the battle for the liberation of the body had started some years earlier. In the summer of 1964 Rudi Gernreich had launched a topless bathing suit which consisted of shorts with a couple of thin shoulder straps. It was seen for the first time on an American bather who was arrested by the police as she came out of the water and charged with indecent exposure. Copious press coverage of the event ensured that pictures of her naked breasts were sent all around the world.

There were wild protests against the topless fashion in the USA, and demonstrations in many places against the sale of topless bathing suits. Women's clubs and church circles were particularly active in their condemnation. When topless bathing suits were presented at fashion shows in Europe the reaction was less puritanical. The Church warned against the topless fashion in Italy and Spain, but two-piece bathing suits such as the bikini were already banned on public beaches there. Some shop-owners stocked the new fashion but often without much enthusiasm, believing it was just a passing fad.[2]

Rudi Gernreich himself, speaking on American television, observed with foresight, 'It may well be a bit much now, but just wait. In a couple of years, topless bikinis will be a reality and regarded as perfectly natural.'[3]

(opposite) Moulded bra in flesh-coloured Lycra by Warner and fishnet tights in soft stretch material, 1965.

Penelope Tree in see-through silk blouse and Bermuda shorts by Yves Saint-Laurent, 1968.

Topless bathing costume, 1964.

When the two Danish fashion firms Carli Gry and Wiki presented the topless fashion for the first time in Denmark, the police, in deciding whether or not to ban the show in advance, wanted to know how the fashion would be presented. The topless bathing suits were to be worn by a former stripper; she was to appear with five other models who would be wearing more modest bathing suits, and the arrangers guaranteed that the stripper would not cause any offence.[4]

Fashion historian Broby-Johansen, who had written several articles in the 1950s warning against the harmful effects of the 'torpedo brassière' on the breasts, wrote in 1964 that the topless look, which liberated the breasts, should be taken seriously and was an expression of the liberation of modern women – a new phase in the battle of the sexes. 'A new generation of women is coming forward from the swing clubs and the anti-nuclear marches. They won't be fooled. They are demonstrating the genuine article,' proclaimed Broby.[5]

His jubilation was somewhat premature. It was another five years before women were ready to get rid of their bras completely and Broby was justified in writing his newspaper article 'Obituary for the Bra' in May 1969.

The naked look really caught on at the beginning of the 1970s, for men as well as for women. It became commonplace for women to be seen topless on the beach and nakedness was, therefore, no longer a provocation. Moreover, breasts hold less erotic interest when exposed than when wholly or partly concealed.

Underwear was reduced to the bare minimum in the 1970s: the ideal was a natural appearance. Bikini briefs became fashionable, one of the smallest types being the tanga, which appeared in 1973.

These were hard times for both *haute couture* and the corset industry, which felt a decline in the demand for both prestige clothes and corsetry. New thinking was necessary if the French fashion houses and manufacturers of underwear wanted to survive the crisis caused by the new norms for clothing. The fashion houses began to produce ready-to-wear clothes which, together with accessories and perfume, were sold from their affiliated 'boutiques' in parallel with their *haute couture* lines.

It came as a shock to the manufacturers of underwear that many women got rid of their bras completely, thus demonstrating that the bust did not perhaps need the support the manufacturers had for years been saying it did. But when bra manufacturers began in 1972 to produce 'invisible' bras, which met the demand for a natural shape and also gave full-busted women the support they needed, bra sales again began to pick up.

Matching sets of briefs and soft bras became fashionable. Some sets also

Bra and briefs in nylon crêpe with printed pattern by Mary Quant, 1974.

Soft 'invisible' bra by Huit, 1973.
Body-stocking in soft flesh-coloured Lycra net by Warner, 1965.

included tights. Some of the underwear was made of cotton, often co-loured, or coloured nylon crêpe, sometimes with cartoon designs. Mary Quant's designs were popular. The crêpe sets were not particularly dur-able; they ran just as easily as crêpe stockings, but the price per set was very low.

Another well-fitting and rather more expensive type of underwear was made of polyester or nylon combined with Lycra; it fitted the body snugly and accentuated natural shapes. These fabrics were used for a lot of under-wear by Vassarette and Triumph, which also launched the 'One Size' bra, which stretched to fit. White, black or flesh were the most popular colours for this type.

The bodystocking became very popular in the 1970s. It is a modern type of corselet made of soft, elastic material, which fits snugly to the body, almost like a second skin. It is fastened in the crotch by hooks and eyes or press-studs. The bodystocking was introduced in autumn 1964 by the Warner Corset Company in the USA. In flesh-coloured Lycra net it was a revolutionary innovation, offering a lighter and more comfortable form of corsetry.

Soft and comfortable underwear, either completely plain or with a little lace, was the most popular type in the 1970s. From 1973 the exclusive French underwear firm Aubade began showing its collections of sophisticated underwear, with and without lace. Hanne Pasquier and her husband, Claude Pasquier, founded Aubade and have been responsible for the ideas for and design of the firm's output. Today Aubade is one of the most popular brands of underwear. In 1973, however, many women refused to wear sexy or decorative underwear, associating it with seduction and eroticism, which were the new taboos. Aubade's feminine, lacy underwear did not really catch on until the late 1970s, when the female body was again in focus, but this time in a more self-confident and liberated mode than before.

Fashion in the 1970s was characterized by many different styles. Many of the existing norms for clothing had been rejected during the 1960s and clothes became more a symbol of the different lifestyles they were expected to represent. The fashion industry took inspiration partly from the dress styles of fringe and anti-establishment groups and partly from the hippie movement.

Hippie culture was an alternative movement opposed to the materialism and consumerism of modern Western society. It started in San Francisco but spread to many other places during the 1960s. Hippies were often young, mainly middle-class intellectuals in search of new values and lifestyles. In the late 1960s, the hippies expressed more vociferously than any

The Gossard Wonderbra became an icon of the 1970s.

Thin body-stockings
in black and white
nylon crêpe, 1969.

other group their opposition to American involvement in the Vietnam War. The hippie style was initially a nostalgic attempt to get back to the 'natural' and 'genuine' – an anti-fashion and anti-establishment style, typified by unconventional behaviour and demeanour, long hair and multi-coloured, loose, unisex clothes. Hippies showed their solidarity with poor and repressed groups by wearing African and Oriental clothes, Mexican ponchos and Indian headbands. By the early 1970s the fashion industry had taken hippie clothing, combined it with an admixture of folk ingredients from other cultures and transformed it into a luxury style.

The long hair and multi-coloured clothes of the hippies were – with the exception of skirts for women – largely devoid of sex-specific characteristics. It was the first time there had been a feminization of men's clothes since the beginning of the nineteenth century, when decoration of their clothing had fallen from favour. It had been taboo for men to wear feminine clothing, but not for women to wear masculine clothes. When women had first begun to wear trousers for sport at the end of the nineteenth century they had been jeered at, but gradually trousers became acceptable as women's wear. Hippie clothes challenged these norms and helped to make sex-specific clothing obsolete.

Unisex clothing became fashionable at the beginning of the 1970s. Even underwear was produced in the same shapes for men and women, and the fly in men's underpants disappeared.

Hippie parade in Haight
Ashbury, San Francisco, 1967.

Unisex underwear, 1974.

Jeans are probably the one item of clothing that has had the most variable meaning in recent times. American jeans first appeared in Europe in the 1950s, where they were mostly worn by teenagers as leisure clothing. In the 1960s they became the symbol of youth rebellion against the conservatism and class overtones of the older generation's clothes. Worn, overwashed jeans, often patched with different colours, became an expression of a new, alternative lifestyle; matched with clothes from surplus stores, cast-offs and homemade items, they became an element in the 'uniform' of the anti-culture. Jeans spread to many other social groups in the 1970s, becoming leisure clothes for the whole family and thereby losing their meaning as protest clothes. Jeans are now worn by just about everyone, regardless of sex, age or social class.

When they first appeared jeans were an expression of a 'free' and anti-fashion attitude with which the women's movement could identify. Women did not want to continue to be kept in the role of sex objects, but neither did they want to dress as though they were men. Jeans, being neither overtly feminine nor typically masculine, fitted the bill admirably. But are these trousers actually comfortable?

In his essay 'Thinking with the Hips' (1976), Umberto Eco reflected – after having bought a pair of jeans – on the dialectic between repression and liberation:

The trousers did not hurt, but I could certainly feel them. However elastic they were, I could feel a kind of armour around the lower half of my body . . . I noticed that my movements, the way I walked, turned round, sat down and hurried had become different . . . An experience which is nothing new for women.

All of their clothing has been intended to make them act in a certain way: high heels, corsets, stiffened bras, etc. . . .

An apparent symbol of freedom and equality with men, those jeans that fashion now requires women to wear are yet another of the traps of Oppression. They do not liberate the body; on the contrary, they subject it to a new etiquette. Jeans lock the body into another form of armour, which, because the clothes are apparently not 'feminine', does not look like armour.[6]

Eco recognized something important about jeans: they demonstrate the fact that liberation is a relative term which we experience very differently in time and space. Jeans do not appear to be repressive – they are relaxed and informal and convey a message of 'freedom' – yet, within limits, they follow the mutability of fashion. Jeans were supposed to be worn very tight in the 1970s: to achieve this, the wearer put them on while they were wet and let them dry on the body. The result was that they gripped the body like armour, the zip could be done up only with difficulty, they were uncomfortable and there is some evidence that they were also detrimental to male fertility. Thus jeans, the archetypal pro-freedom, anti-fashion

Jeans were practical and were popular for both sexes, but they were not always comfortable to wear.

item, became, paradoxically, a fashion item and instrument of oppression.

Women's libbers rejected the use of make-up. They wore jeans or dungarees, a T-shirt and a coloured cloth on their head. This gave them a feeling of freedom and solidarity with other women, but not, however, with women who presented themselves differently. Women who attended meetings wearing a dress and make-up, though just as keen to share common problems with their sisters, often felt unwelcome. In the feminists' opinion there was only one form of women's liberation – a total rejection of the female image. Many women were frightened by the regi-

Women's Festival in Copenhagen, August 1976.

mentation of the women's movement and rejected the 'anti-man' tone expressed by its most radical members.

In her book *The Second Stage*, Betty Friedan, one of the pioneers of the modern American women's movement, openly recognized its mistakes and tried to formulate new possibilities for women – together with men. She regretted the excesses of some women in the movement who in the late 1960s were labelled as bra-burning man-haters and who attracted the scorn of the leaders in *Newsweek* and *Time*:

But that's not what we meant, not at all. For us, with our roots in the middle American mainstream and our own 1950s families, equality and the personhood of women never meant destruction of the family, repudiation of marriage and motherhood, or implacable sexual war against men. That 'bra-burning' note shocked and outraged us, and we knew it was wrong – personally and politically – though we never said so, then, as loudly as we should have.[7]

The image against which Betty Friedan and other feminists rebelled was that of a woman totally fulfilled in her role as homemaker, mother and pretty wife. In the economic boom after the Second World War the feminine ideal, which Betty Friedan called the 'feminine myth', became a barrier preventing women from realizing their own personality. They were caught in the limiting role of mythologized femininity and the social demands on women to conform with the ideal image of men – the enemy.

Dressed for work, 1976. Narrow pin-striped three-piece suit in a masculine cut. Long trousers for women were now acceptable for work.

The 1960s and the beginning of the 1970s marked a period of economic growth, wealth and demand for labour. Great numbers of women became active on the labour market and many stayed at work even after they had children, which meant that they effectively had two full-time jobs. The division of labour in most homes had not changed significantly, despite the fact that more women went out to work. The economic crisis came in 1973/4 and competition for jobs became extremely intense. This had an effect on women's appearance and particularly on their clothes, which became rather masculine – a kind of symbol of equality. The very young ideal with her miniskirts, 'hot pants' or trousers gave way to a more mature ideal dressed mainly in suits, trousers and dresses in a rather severe classical style.

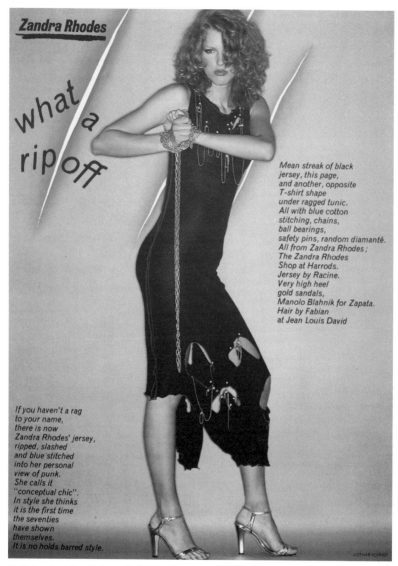

Zandra Rhodes

what a rip off

Mean streak of black
jersey, this page,
and another, opposite
T-shirt shape
under ragged tunic.
All with blue cotton
stitching, chains,
ball bearings,
safety pins, random diamanté.
All from Zandra Rhodes;
The Zandra Rhodes
Shop at Harrods.
Jersey by Racine.
Very high heel
gold sandals,
Manolo Blahnik for Zapata.
Hair by Fabian
at Jean Louis David

If you haven't a rag
to your name,
there is now
Zandra Rhodes' jersey,
ripped, slashed
and blue stitched
into her personal
view of punk.
She calls it
"conceptual chic".
In style she thinks
it is the first time
the seventies
have shown
themselves.
It is no holds barred style.

Punk-inspired dress in jersey by Zandra Rhodes, 1977.

Changes in attitude and dress occurred both within the mainstream and on the fringes. The punk subculture arose in the summer of 1976 in the working-class areas of several British cities, but the punks had a wider class base than other groups. They protested against high unemployment and the shortage of housing, which particularly hit the young. Their chosen symbolic forms of protest were deliberately deviant and shocking. Their clothes consisted of items taken out of their usual context and rearranged in new combinations to destroy the old meanings and create the new.[8] Punks sometimes dressed in plastic or leather clothes; or they might take items from a middle-class wardrobe – military and school uniforms, for example – and wear them covered with graffiti; often, too, they wore rags, tatters and discards. As decoration they slung dog-collars and toilet chains around their necks and and wore safety-pins in pierced cheeks, noses or ears. They used grotesque make-up and dyed their hair strong colours.

'Clothed in chaos, they produced Noise ... a noise which made [no] sense ... beyond the horror circus antics, a divided and unequal society was being eloquently condemned,' wrote Dick Hebdige in his book *Sub-culture: The Meaning of Style*.[9] In previous subcultures the boys had predominated; in punk culture, by contrast, girls too were visible. Their deviant and provocative clothing denoted a clear distancing from the pre-valent aesthetic values and a rejection of the traditional view of femininity. Punk was an anti-fashion style, but, unlike the cult of the 'natural' of the hippies and feminists, it chose an artificial mode of expressing genuine principles.

The commercial fashion industry has always 'stolen' or imitated ele-ments of both subcultures and anti-cultures. Once this happened to punk, the style was immediately disarmed of its original symbolic value. No longer a form of protest, punk style nevertheless spread quickly and continued to be used by young people to signal their difference from the established and the conventional. It rejected the natural look and, though it did not stress eroticism, the deviant and provocative clothing, decoration and body painting marked a new awareness of physicality, which inspired the fashion industry to push out the existing barriers of acceptability and create a renewal.

A new movement in art, postmodernism, began to make itself felt at the end of the 1970s, representing a clash with the natural, pure and simple forms of functionalism. For the first time in decades, decoration allied with form became an important element in architecture, furniture and fashion. In line with this, from mid-1977 the feminine ideal began to assume new aspects. The female body had been desexualized. Now it was decked out in such symbols of femininity as high-heeled shoes, nylon stockings, suspender belts and garters. During the ensuing underwear re-volution, the simple, smooth forms that had been the fashion until then were replaced by sexy, decorative, silk underwear, and sales boomed of ro-mantically feminine underwear and nightwear in shiny satin with lace.

10 New Physical Awareness and Greater Self-Confidence *c*. 1978–1990s

Fashion in the 1980s was not one single phenomenon but a collection of coexisting tendencies. Common to most of these, however, although expressed in various ways, was the concept of physical awareness. In the past, the dress or, rather, the corsetry had shaped the body to the shape that was the prevalent ideal of the time and the culture. The body had to be shaped and decorated with external symbols of the owner's social status. In the 1960s and especially in the 1970s many of the previous clothing norms were rejected and clothes came, above all, to denote various lifestyles.

The two main tendencies in 1980s fashion – stylish, classic citywear and relaxed, sporty leisurewear – both emphasized a dynamic and fit body as the basis for clothing. Artificial devices to beautify the figure or change its shape were dispensed with, but as the body was still supposed to look natural, it had itself to become the object of fixation and idealization. The body itself, rather than its clothing, became the significant means of communication, and this meant that greater demands were made of the body's aesthetics.

In the 1980s people took part, as never before, in sport, fitness classes, power training sessions, running and other types of exercise, all as part of the quest to 'keep in shape' – an expression often used to mean keeping the body supple, youthful and in good condition, and avoiding decline despite advancing age. Beauty became synonymous with a youthful, slim (but not thin), fit and suntanned body. For women this also included firm, rather full breasts, a slim waist and narrow hips. People no longer perfected their bodies with beauty aids or lived with them undisguised in all their 'naturalness'; instead, they worked to shape their own bodies to match up to the ideal.

The shape of the body was an expression not just of an aesthetic sense but also of strength and self-confidence – attributes that have been of vital importance in Western competitive society. Many companies had arrangements with fitness centres whereby employees could keep them-

Pretty lace bodystocking by Marie Jo, 1988.

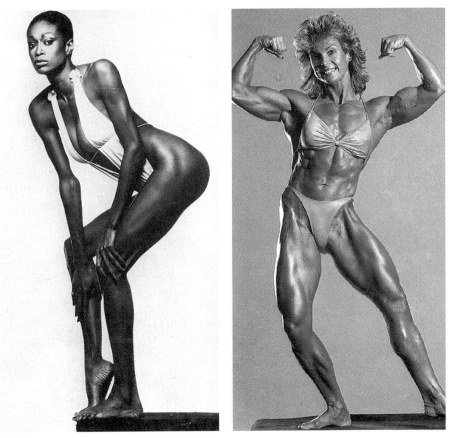

Athletic Sheila Ming in a bathing suit by John Bates, 1978.

Mary Roberts, Female Bodybuilding World Champion, 1985, epitomizes body worship.

selves in shape, with a view to generating a feeling of greater well-being and a greater capacity for work. Fitness centres began to open up all over the Western world. Many of their clients were working men and women aged between twenty and forty, who wanted to be seen to radiate dynamism, efficiency, strength and self-control. But a lot of time and money were required to build up and maintain the ideal body, which demanded not only exercise and muscle training but also healthy food (which costs more than 'junk' food) and, since a suntan was part of the aesthetic, regular trips to the solarium.

Since human beings can never achieve perfection, only mannequins could represent the ideal – the perfect woman in moulded plastic. The female body ideal of the 1980s was a refinement of the realistic body ideal of the 1970s, but even more precisely shaped to be as 'natural' as possible, down to the smallest detail. She was tall, slim and supple with long, well-shaped but not muscular legs. There is something sensually challenging about this body – liberated, self-confident, but also exceptionally idealized. This kind of body itself lends shape to the clothes; it needs no support of any kind, and on it clothes become a kind of decoration.

Hindsgaul Mannequins is one of the world's leading manufacturers of mannequins. Each model they develop is given a name, but the type can be changed by varying the make-up and hairstyle. This versatility was perfectly in tune with the multiplicity of fashion images available in the 1980s. After the mid-1980s all the female mannequins had a different look about them: they seemed, as it were, to stand more firmly on their own two feet, and to radiate more self-confidence and sensuality.

From about the same time another type of model began to appear alongside the very lifelike mannequins that constituted the bulk of production in the decade. This new type represented a very simplified form,

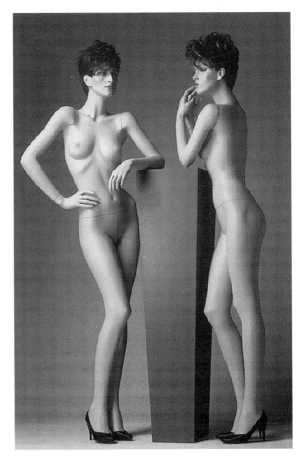

Tall, self-confident ideal women by Hindsgaul Manne-quins. 'Sandra' mannequin from 1987.

devoid of any of the definition that could be denoted by, for example, make-up or hairstyle. The body was just as accurately modelled as that of the lifelike type, but all the models had the same short, moulded hair and the same vague facial features. Their featureless anonymity was underlined by their colour, which was the same all over. Most were white, but some were gold, silver or bronze-coloured, some even green or brown. In this model the body was pure form.

In an exhibition called *Stars of French Fashion* in 1988, the Museum of Decorative Art in Copenhagen exhibited contemporary fashions on completely white mannequins without make-up and with moulded hairstyles. The mannequins did not draw attention away from the clothes, but helped to create an exciting contrast. The same effect was used at a retrospective exhibition of clothes by Yves Saint-Laurent at the Metropolitan Museum of Art in New York in 1983, but in this case the heads of the models were covered with jersey fabric, which almost erased their features altogether. The body and the clothing alone denoted female fashion.

Earlier, around 1978, a two-pronged tendency had developed. On the one hand, there was a greater polarization between feminine and masculine clothes; on the other, women began to wear items of male clothing combined with female. This contrast was characteristic of women's dress in the 1980s. The masculine suit was widely adopted by women as the working outfit or citywear. Men's jackets with lapels and padded shoulders

Elegant, broad-shouldered men's jacket, tight skirt and top by Yves Saint-Laurent, 1989.

were teamed with long trousers or skirts; for contrast, elegant silk or imitation silk blouses with bows at the neck were worn. High-heeled shoes were again in fashion, now also worn with trousers.

The change of mood was most obvious in underwear. Underwear had been reduced to relatively few small, practical articles of clothing, until the late 1970s, when interest again began to grow in sophisticated lingerie in shiny satin with lace. 'There must be some lace' was the cautious headline in an advertisement by Triumph in 1978. Lace and frills soon appeared in abundance as decoration on underwear. The renewed interest in feminine and sexy underwear did not mean that the figure-controlling symbols of femininity rejected by many women ten years previously were taken up again. The new type of underwear was not designed to shape the body to a specific ideal: it was body decoration pure and simple.

Many of the articles of underwear that appeared at the end of the 1970s had not been seen for years; they now enjoyed a renaissance in silk, crêpe-de-chine and satin, or in the cheaper imitation satin, polyester and polyamide. Short chemises and camisoles with matching bikini briefs, tangas or 'French knickers' (wide-legged knickers that had gone out of fashion in the 1940s) became popular again. Cami-knickers – camisole and knickers in one – especially popular in the 1920s and 1930s now reappeared in a new elegant form, this time called a teddy, with hooks and eyes in the crotch.

The tight-fitting bodystocking was still in use, but towards the end of the 1970s it was the feminine, romantic and sexy underwear that particularly appealed to women, while the growth of physical awareness through the 1980s markedly increased sales of bodystockings and other tight-fitting articles of underwear that accentuated the shape of the body.

The bra also made a comeback, but in more varied forms. The new bras met the requirement for a natural bustline as well as giving the necessary support. Like other underwear, however, many bras became extremely decorative, thus acquiring an aesthetic function over and above their practicality. In the early 1980s most bras were soft, although some had underwiring and there were three-quarter-cup bras for wear with low necklines. During the decade the sale of underwired bras grew so sharply that by 1989 such sales accounted for about half the total for all bras.

Bras were mostly sold as part of a set with matching briefs or as part of a whole sophisticated ensemble. The individual parts could, of course, be bought separately, but manufacturers played on the consumers' desire to have elegantly matching outfits. Towards the end of the 1980s many underwear series were sold with matching lace-top stockings. The range included hold-ups, which were held in place by an elasticated band at the top, and ordinary stockings, which would be worn with suspenders. The

Camisole and French knickers in satin polyester with broad lace edging, 1978.

Teddy with waist ties by Aubade, 1987.

most popular colours were white, black and ivory, but many firms launched their collections in exciting new colours each time. For example, Ming blue, grey and pink were the main colours in the 1986 underwear collection of the exclusive French firm Aubade, and in 1989 satin-look underwear in dusty violet was shown alongside black and white ranges.

Sexy, sophisticated underwear sold extraordinarily well from the end of the 1970s and well into the 1980s, as can be seen from the doubling in size of department stores' lingerie departments. The very feminine silk and satin lace underwear mostly appealed to adult women, while younger

Matching underwired bra, high-waisted briefs, suspender belt and stockings: sophisticated lace underwear set by Marie Jo, 1989.

women preferred simple, more sporty, cotton underwear. However, it is not sensible to generalize any further about women's wear during this period, since there were so many different fashions, giving women unprecedented freedom to express their individuality and versatility in the way they looked. People's clothes no longer clearly indicated their identification with a role, but became a variable means of expressing different facets of the same person. Dressing became a kind of game with optional role changes to suit the wearer's mood.

Barthes frowned on this kind of role changing, saying it was superficial and represented a 'depersonalization' that put the wearer's identity at risk.[1] Barthes's worry might be justified if human identity changed with a changed appearance; but the use of varying modes of expression to create different looks should perhaps be welcomed as a sign of demasking and the breaking down of boundaries and preconceptions, rather than of superficial masking.

With their greater self-confidence many women dared to show several sides of themselves – including the erotic. This does not mean that women who wore sexy underwear were more liberated; nor, on the other hand, can the trend be interpreted as a backlash, a backward step for wo-

Body-hugging underwear. Top and briefs in cotton Lycra by Pont Neuf, 1988.

Body-hugging fashion. Top and leggings with corset by Chantal Thomass, 1988.

men's liberation, as many people saw it. Feminine underwear did not signal a return to traditional sex roles; on the contrary, it was, I believe, a sign that many women had become sufficiently self-confident and strong to dress in feminine clothes without fear of being labelled as sex objects.

Nevertheless, whatever equality women had achieved in other areas, the business world was still male-dominated and to participate in it women had to tone down their feminine side and wear neutral, classical male clothing. The outfit with a jacket was one of the most chic and popular fashions for women, denoting initiative and dynamism. And, like the tailored jacket and skirt of the Belle Epoque in the 1890s, worn by working women and as a chic outfit by the upper classes, the 1980s suit was softened by the addition of feminine items. In both periods masculine clothing was worn as a sign of equality, but the feminine overtones were added as a way of giving multiple signals.

With the growing physical awareness that took hold from the mid-1980s, a more body-hugging fashion appeared, in parallel with the classical jacket, for both young and more mature women. The tight clothes accentuated the female form, putting the body in the spotlight, and becoming more daring, provocative and erotic. Although their gender was

208

thus emphasized, women were in no way using this to send a message that they would tolerate any kind of limitation on them because of their sex.

The artificial elastic fibre Lycra was an essential ingredient of these tight-fitting clothes. Designers such as Jean-Paul Gaultier and Katharine Hamnett were among the first in the 1980s to make body-hugging tube dresses, leggings, blouses and short skirts from elasticated fabrics, especially a cotton–Lycra mix. Underwear also became more tight-fitting and the difference between outerwear and underwear became less pronounced. A lace-trimmed camisole might often be used as a top for evening wear or as decoration under a loose blouse. When the rock star Madonna appeared on stage dressed in a lace bustier towards the end of the 1980s, bras, bra-tops and bustiers became acceptable as visible outerwear, and bustiers in particular were soon being worn in all shapes and guises together with trousers, skirts or a more elegant suit.

Jacket, bustier and short skirt in black leather, 1989.

Madonna in extreme corset designed by Jean-Paul Gaultier.

Body-stocking used as visible top under a suit, 1988.

Gaultier has designed most of Madonna's characteristic and provocative costumes: bras, bustiers and extreme corsets with conical cups and long suspenders. Madonna loves to shock and to appear sexually aggressive and challenging; at the same time, she makes fun of female underwear and presents a parody of femininity, which helps to break new ground for a mode of female expression.

The body-hugging bodystocking again became highly fashionable, sometimes worn as a top together with other underwear. Bodystockings were mostly made of cotton Lycra or lace with Lycra, both of which are soft and comfortable and accentuate the shape of the body. Bodystockings and bra-tops appealed to many women, especially young ones. Underwear had lost its intimacy and become visible body decoration.

Sports and leisure wear was the other main strand in 1980s fashion. Track suits were the great fashion idea from around 1979, initially worn mainly for jogging and exercise, but later as casual clothing for men, women and children of all ages. The actress Jane Fonda was a leading

Jane Fonda demonstrating how effectively her workout programmes can keep the body slim and supple – even when you have turned fifty.

figure in the movement to develop and maintain beautiful, supple and healthy bodies. Her Workout programmes communicated her belief that any woman can achieve this goal quickly and effectively by combining vigorous exercise and healthy eating:

The aim is to build up strength and develop suppleness ... There is no doubt that this programme will give your body new shape and burn off some of those fatty deposits and develop tautness in muscles you didn't even know you had. You will begin to feel fit, physically and mentally. But you have to make up your mind to work out regularly and intensively, eat properly and get enough sleep.[2]

Although this regime is ostensibly designed simply for beauty and health, it is probably equally important as an expression of self-control.

In Western society, overweight women are stigmatized not just for their appearance, which is thought to be ungainly and unattractive, but also for their perceived lack of self-control. The impression given by a fit body is not least one of strength and self-control. In the fitness studio or at the gym, women seem also to find it important to wear the 'right' gear. Skin-tight leotards in shiny, elastic fabrics accentuate the firm, sleek lines of the body – and equally reveal any superfluous fat.

The body has to a greater degree than ever before become an outer shell, the shape and appearance of which can be changed. Moreover, society's demands have changed and many people believe that their chances are enhanced, not only in the context of personal relationships but also on the labour market, if they look younger and more attractive. The mass media constantly reinforce these perceptions and the aspiration to be, or at least to look, young and vital.

But why live with dissatisfaction if the breasts nature gave you are too small or have sagged after childbirth, or if your stomach has become flabbier, when you can buy youth and firmness and re-create your body so that it is acceptable again? Facelifts and other forms of cosmetic surgery have been common for years among American film stars and others whose looks are their fortune. But in the 1980s, increasing numbers of ordinary people of both sexes began to opt for the same course. Men often feel that their professional position depends on a youthful appearance. Most cosmetic surgery is still performed on women, although the more major operations carry a certain degree of risk. On average, more women are dissatisfied with their faces and bodies than men; and they are prepared to invest a lot of money, time and effort on operations to achieve an appearance that comes closer to the ideal.

In the USA and Europe breast operations and liposuction are the most common operations for women, while men tend to have operations on their nose or to reduce heavy eyelids or bags under the eyes. All cosmetic surgery is expensive. In the last decade, many film stars have shown off their pumped-up, enlarged breasts, thus probably making many women with small or slack breasts feel inadequate, some to the extent of deciding to have surgery.

In breast enlargement operations silicone was in the past injected directly into the breast, but it had a tendency to leak out, often with serious consequences. Then silicone implants were developed and inserted into the breast, either under the breast or immediately under the nipple. However, these implants can develop a hard coating that makes the breasts hard too. Doctors can 'break' the coating, but usually only by performing another operation. If the patient massages the breast thoroughly every day for several years, she can reduce the risk that this hard coating may develop, but some women simply have a propensity to develop it, whatever measures they take. The operation can also significantly diminish feeling in the breast and reduce or even destroy the woman's ability to breastfeed. These problems are more common with operations to reduce the size of

Joan Collins has maintained a youthful appearance into middle age.

the breasts by removing breast tissue. Such surgery is also more complex and more expensive, although it is now undergone less frequently, mainly because the feminine ideal is large-busted. Currently most models have full breasts, either because their natural endowment has brought them the opportunity to be successful in this field or because they have had surgery to enhance their bust size.

Liposuction is a method by which unwanted fat is removed from various parts of the body, mostly the thighs, hips and stomach in women. The expense depends on the areas from which the fat is to be removed. Moreover, there is no guarantee that fat will not build up again in the same places.

Facelifts are also expensive and, like most other cosmetic operations, give only a temporary extension of youth: they often have to be repeated some years later. Most women used to have their first facelift around the age of fifty. Nowadays, some start as early as forty. Most cosmetic surgeons advise their patients to have a maximum of two facelifts, otherwise the face is likely to end up looking very stiff and artificial. There is something tragic about many of these faces, in which the eyes often reveal advancing age.

Cosmetic surgery is rapidly becoming more popular, almost certainly because of the tendency in Western society to see only the negative aspects of ageing and to view the decline into old age as a threat. For many, surgery

The American super-model Naomi Campbell showing her bust in a feminine dress by Azzedine Alaïa, 1993.

is merely an extension of the process of clinging on to youth and beauty by other means, such as dyeing the hair, wearing make-up, having teeth straightened, exercise and bodybuilding. Nor is it any longer just the wealthy who opt for cosmetic surgery. There are women who save up for years or borrow money so that they can afford a facelift or new breasts. Clinics rightly turn down some requests for surgery, however, if clients

Gitte Stallone Nielsen has never tried to hide the fact that her bust is not real – quite the opposite.

seem to have an unrealistic expectation of the result of a cosmetic operation. Many women are pleased with the way they look after cosmetic surgery, despite the pain and the expense of it, but others are unfortunately bound to be disappointed. How is this rush to cosmetic surgery to be interpreted? Is it, sadly, evidence that some women feel that they do not measure up to the ideal of the strong, self-confident female?

Among other things, women's liberation in the 1970s encouraged women to take control of their bodies and to learn to accept them as they were instead of trying to alter them to fit the current ideal of beauty. This aim has not been realized in the 1980s and 1990s. The female body has been released from constricting clothing, but it has not been exempted from idealization. This does not necessarily mean that women have given up the struggle for freedom and equality, but rather that the liberation of women and their bodies is being pursued and expressed in other ways.

There are clear differences between the shapeless, liberated tomboy ideal of the 1920s, the 'natural', naked but non-erotic look of the 1970s and the very feminine ideal of the 1980s, created both by the growing cult of body awareness and by the increased self-confidence of women. All three modes signal a form of emancipation, but each expresses that concept in a different way.

Nowadays a pretty bra can be visible under a jacket; advertisement in English *Vogue*, 1987.

The current very feminine ideal, with its emphasis on the bust – and on its beautiful packaging – arouses conflicting attitudes. A number of feminists regard this fixation on the bust as a new form of oppression of women, which, as before, aims at turning women into objects. On the other hand, many other women, especially the younger generation, are tired of this perpetual harping on about equality and sex roles. Of course there should be equality of opportunity and conditions for all, they would argue, but that does not mean that the differences between the sexes could or should disappear.

Linda Andersen, joint founder of Copenhagen's High School for Women, believes that many young female university students today find it difficult to identify with the focus of the women's liberation movement up till now. As she says, they are actually more interested in studying the differences between the sexes than in pursuing equality at all costs:

Their apparent lack of interest in and resistance to women-centred forms of expression should not be taken to prove that young women are attracted to a more traditional female identity and a more traditional way of life; rather they betoken a desire to discover their own mode of expression and their own standpoint . . .

The young people of today have had a childhood which, on the one hand, has not really deflected them from their desire to become 'real' men and women – if we are to judge by the mirror of fashion, which flatters young women who use cosmetics and wear extremely feminine clothes and young men who wear suits and ties. On the other hand, it is a childhood that has perhaps given them a slightly different system of values from that of their parents and encouraged them to expect more space in their lives for interplay and contrast between the sexes.[3]

Young people's visions for the future are hardly sex-specific. Both sexes expect to have a career and at the same time to have children, a home and a good family life – with joint effort. It has become more usual to show each other consideration and a higher degree of emotional engagement in relationships. Although much progress has been made towards evening out the pattern of sex roles, it has become more acceptable for both sexes to play on their sexual charisma. Women of today expect to be able to show off their female forms without being regarded purely as sex objects; but they realize that this requires them to be more than physical beings.

Sex came back into the picture in the 1980s. However, there was a contradictory tendency, especially in the first half of the decade, to portray women's bodies in such a way that they exuded sex and yet were not intended to give free rein to men's sexual fantasies. This ambiguity arose mostly because the question of sex roles was still a very sensitive area and women took offence on behalf of their gender with very little provocation.

An advertisement from the French firm Aubade in 1983 showing a male hand resting provocatively on a woman's bare thigh caused great offence. The advertisement was censored by the French minister Yvette Roudy, who tried to ban advertisements that were sexually discriminatory or, in the case of advertisements for underwear, could be interpreted as erotic or seductive. On the other hand, advertisers were perfectly at liberty to promote sexy and feminine underwear for wives or girlfriends to male purchasers.

Shops advertise this kind of underwear – as 'the gift from him to her' – especially fiercely around Christmas, consciously playing on the erotic

The advertisement from Aubade which many women found discriminatory when it appeared in 1983.

aspect and men's hopes that their fantasies will be fulfilled by the giving of such gifts. For the rest of the year women buy the lovely underwear for themselves.

The relationship between the sexes has obviously also changed. Women no longer see men as enemies and oppressors who have to be fought. That battle is over. But there are probably still quite a number of men who are uncertain how to react to the strong and self-confident women who signal a heightened physicality and sexuality and at the same time refuse to be regarded as sex objects.

The ultra-feminine ideal that caught on around 1978 elicited numerous protests from some in the women's movement who, ten years earlier, had helped get rid of many of the symbols of femininity then being reintroduced. But the attitude to female modes of expression changed in the course of the 1980s. The enormous boom in the underwear industry over this decade was primarily due to the new confidence and self-awareness of women. It was principally women themselves who bought the feminine and sexy underwear. At the end of 1989 a new, curvaceous feminine ideal with a full bust appeared on the fashion scene, in keeping with the tendency to accentuate female sex identity. Women proudly showed off their attributes, demonstrating their newfound readiness to express themselves in a feminine way with also a little more warmth and eroticism.

The big-busted feminine ideal arrived on the scene in the same year as the bra celebrated its 100th birthday. The media marked the occasion with the usual display of naked or half-naked breasts. The fashion industry is not much influenced by this kind of advertising event – there are other much more important things to take into account. On the other hand, the increased attention given to breasts certainly had an effect on the already remarkable sales of bras. And this renewed focus on the bust and its incorporation into the feminine ideal in the late 1980s and early 1990s, in both the fashion and the advertising industries, could not have happened if it had not been for the enhanced self-awareness of women.

The rate at which feminine ideals are generated has not diminished, nor has the demand for women to be attractive, even though women have achieved higher status in most areas of society; on the contrary, the idealization and reshaping of the body are more widespread today than in the past. But women have gained much greater influence on the shaping of the current ideal images, and similarly greater opportunities to decide over their own bodies and create their own individuality. In addition, women have started in the past ten years to make the same demands of men to be attractive as men have always made of women. The male body has become a sex object and a more obvious subject for idealization; and it is increasingly used as an eyecatcher in advertising.

Attractive lace body-stocking by Aubade – pure body decoration, 1992.

Corset and briefs by Rosy, 1991.

Calvin Klein design for men, 1993.

Modern young women have on the whole discarded some unnecessary limitations on their existence and future self-realization, and this has made them happier to be women than were their predecessors. For their greater freedom, equality and self-confidence, they are indebted to women of previous generations, especially in the last century and a half, who blazed a trail with their strenuous efforts on behalf of the female sex.

References

Introduction

1 Simone de Beauvoir, *The Second Sex* (Harmondsworth, 1974), trans. H. M. Parshley, p. 283
2 Werner Schmalenbach, 'Kraft og Mådehold – Den sorte afrikanske kunsts æstetik' (Power and Moderation – The Aesthetics of Black African Art), in *Louisiana Revy* March 1989; and 'Magi og ritualer i Afrikas kunst' (Magic and Ritual in the Art of Africa), in *Eksotisk Kunst* (Copenhagen, 1970)
3 Roland Barthes, *The Fashion System* (London, 1985), trans. Matthew Ward and Richard Howard
4 Umberto Eco, *La struttura assente*, publ. Lund as *Den Frånvarande Strukturen*, 1971

PART I THE FEMALE PHYSICAL IDEAL

1 *The Status Image*

1 Charles Darwin, *The Voyage of the 'Beagle'* (London, 1972), pp. 183 and 196
2 Margaret Mead, *Male and Female: A Study of the Sexes in a Changing World* (London, 1950)
3 Søren Nanck-Krogh, *Kunsten på kroppen – om tatovering* (*Art on the Body – On Tattooing*) (Copenhagen, 1985)
4 Kirsten Hastrup and Jan Ovesen, *Etnografisk grundbog* (*Basic Ethnography*) (Copenhagen, 1980), p. 274
5 Karen Blixen, 'Daguerreotypes', in *Daguerreotypes and Other Essays*, trans. P. M. Mitchell and W. D. Paden (Chicago, 1979), p. 63
6 Desmond Morris, *Bodywatching* (Jonathan Cape, 1985)
7 Thorstein Veblen, *The Theory of the Leisure Class* (New York, 1899)
8 Jean Baudrillard, *For a Critique of the Political Economy of the Sign*, trans. Charles Levin (Telos Press, 1981), p. 205
9 Roland Barthes, *The Fashion System*
10 J. C. Flügel, *The Psychology of Clothes* (London, 1930)
11 *Tidens Kvinder* (Copenhagen, 1944)
12 *Alt for Damerne* (Copenhagen, 2 May 1989)
13 *Tidens Kvinder* (July 1944)
14 Finn Skårderud, *Sultekunstnerne* (*The Professional Fasters*) (Copenhagen, 1992)
15 Bryan S. Turner, *The Body and Society* (Sage, 1996)
16 Barbara Sichtermann, *Weiblichkeit* (*Femininity*) (Berlin, 1986), p. 58
17 Ibid., p. 59

2 *Morality, Perception of the Body and Aesthetics*

1 Charles Baudelaire, *The Painter of Modern Life and Other Essays*, trans. and ed. Jonathan Mayne (New York, 1986)

2 Choderlos de Laclos, *Les Liaisons Dangereuses*, trans. Dr P. W. K. Stone (Harmondsworth, 1961), pp. 179–80

3 Ibid., p. 188

4 Giacomo Casanova, *Histoire de ma vie* (*History of my Life*)

5 Otto Rosenbach, *Korset og Blegsot* (*Corsets and Anaemia*) (Copenhagen, 1895)

6 E. P. Thompson, 'Time, Work-Discipline and Industrial Capitalism', in *Past and Present*, 38 (London, 1967)

7 Roland Barthes, *Mythologies*, trans. Annette Lavers (London, 1974)

8 David Kunzle, *Fashion and Fetishism* (London, 1982)

9 Michel Foucault, *A History of Sexuality*, trans. Robert Hurley, vol. II (New York, 1986), p. 143

10 Ellen Andersen, *Moden i 1700-årene* (*Fashion in the Eighteenth Century*) (Copenhagen, 1977)

11 Cécil Saint-Laurent, *A History of Women's Underwear* (London, 1986), p. 104

12 David Kunzle, *Fashion and Fetishism*, p. 31

3 *Dress and Fashion*

1 John Stuart Mill, *On Liberty* (originally published 1859), ed. Elizabeth Rapaport (Hackett, 1982), p. 68

2 Sven B. Ek, 'Dräkten i samhället – samhället i dräkten' (Dress in Society – Society in Dress), in *Folkelig Dräkt* (*Popular Dress*), ed. S. Svensson (Lund, 1974), pp. 141–2

3 Elizabeth Ewing, *Dress and Undress* (London, 1986), p. 22

4 L. Kybalova, *Modens Billedleksikon* (*A Pictorial Dictionary of Fashion*) (Copenhagen, 1968), p. 127

5 Umberto Eco, *The Name of the Rose*, trans. William Weaver (London, 1996), p. 252

6 Hartvig Frisch, *Europas Kulturhistorie* (*The Cultural History of Europe*), vol. III (Copenhagen, 1973), p. 112

7 E. H. Gombrich, *The Story of Art* (London, 1995)

8 L. Kybalova, *Modens Billedleksikon*, p. 164

9 Elizabeth Ewing, *Dress and Undress*, p. 22

10 Roland Barthes, 'Histoire et Sociologie du Vêtement', in *Annales*, 3 (1957)

11 Roland Barthes, *The Fashion System*, p. 270

12 Karen Blixen, *Daguerreotypes*, pp. 18–19

13 Charles Baudelaire, *The Painter of Modern Life and Other Essays*

4 *Propagation of the Fashion Ideal*

1 Marce Tarnowska, *Fashion Dolls* (London, 1986)

2 Vyvyan Holland, *Hand-Coloured Fashion Plates 1770–1899* (London, 1988)

3 Birgit Fischer, 'Legedukker og dukkelege' (Dolls and Games), in *Det legede vi med* (*What We Played With*) (Copenhagen, 1982), p. 72

4 Billy Boy, *Barbie* (London, 1987); and catalogue, 1959

5 Jacob Moresco, *Minder far mit Liv* (*Memories from my Life*) (Copenhagen, 1896), p. 96

6 Jean Baudrillard, 'Fashion, or the Enchanting Spectacle of the Code', trans. Iain Hamilton, in *Symbolic Exchange and Death* (Sage, 1993), p. 98

PART II PHYSICAL ALTERATION 1880s–1990s

5 *The Corseted Woman 1880s–c. 1909*

1 Karen Blixen, *Seven Gothic Tales* (Harmondsworth, 1963), pp. 62–3

2 Corset advertisement for Duzaine Hansen in *Nordisk Mønster-Tidende* (*Nordic Pattern Times*) (Copenhagen, 1900)

3 Anne Buck, *Victorian Costume and Costume Accessories* (London, 1984)

4 Article in *Samfundet* (*Society*) (Copenhagen, 12 December 1900)

5   Emile Zola, *Nana*, trans. Douglas Parmée (Oxford, 1992), p. 274

6   Thit Jensen, 'Hvordan Tider Skaber Mennesker' (How Times Create People), in *Kvinder ser i Tidens Spejl* (*Women Looking in the Mirror of Time*) (Copenhagen, 1947), p. 39

7   Frantz Howitz, *Bidrag til en Sundhedslære for Kvinder* (*Contribution to Health Education for Women*) (Copenhagen, 1892), p. 39

8   Edith Rode, 'Glimt fra Halvfemserne' (A Glimpse from the Nineties), in *Kvinder ser i Tidens Spejl*, pp. 55–6

9   Georg Brandes, Foreword to Danish translation of John Stuart Mill's *The Subjection of Women* (Copenhagen, 1979), p. 7

10 John Stuart Mill, *The Subjection of Women* (London, 1970)

11 Astrid Bugge, *Reformdragten i Norge* (*The Reform Dress in Norway*) (Oslo, 1984), p. 5

12 Ibid., p. 6

13 Otto Rosenbach, *Korset og Blegsot* (*Corsets and Anaemia*) (Copenhagen, 1895)

14 Karen Blixen, *On Modern Marriage*, trans. Anne Born (Fourth Estate, 1986), p. 42

15 Frantz Howitz, *Bidrag til en Sundhedslære for Kvinder*, p. 37

16 Article in *Kvinden og Samfundet* (*Women and Society*) (Copenhagen, Danish Women's Society, February 1893), pp. 25–6

17 Marie Luplau, 'Om Cykling for Damer' (Cycling for Women), in *Kvinden og Samfundet* (1894), pp. 6-7

18 Frantz Howitz, *Bidrag til en Sundhedslære for Kvinder*, pp. 34–5

6   *The New Slender Look c. 1910–1929*

1   Olga Hoffmann-Canitz, *Moderne Skønhedspleje* (*Modern Beauty Care*) (Copenhagen, 1917), pp. 61–2

2   Poul Henningsen, 'Kvindemenneske' (The Female of the Species), in *Kulturkampen* (*The Battle for Culture*), 4 (Copenhagen, 1935)

3   *Aftenbladet* (*The Evening Post*) (Copenhagen, 1958)

4   'Vort Uskønne Sommer-Badeliv' (Our Unattractive Summer Beachlife), in *Vore Damer* (*Our Ladies*) (Copenhagen, 1918)

5   Emma Gad, *Takt og Tone* (*Social Etiquette*) (Copenhagen, 1918), pp. 177–8

6   Poul Henningsen, 'Kvinden i ny Belysning' (Women in a New Light), in *Politiken* (Copenhagen, 13 June 1931)

7   Harald Engberg, *Filmen* (*Film*) (Copenhagen, 1939), p. 112

8   Roland Barthes, *Mythologies*

9   Rune Waldekranz, *Filmens Historie* (*The Story of Film*), vol. II (Värnamo, 1986), p. 286

7   *The Soft-Contoured, Slender Body c. 1930–46*

1   James Laver, *Costume and Fashion* (London, 1985), p. 241

2   Elsa Gress, *Fuglefri og fremmed – Erindringsbilleder* (*Free as a Bird and Foreign – Memories*) (Copenhagen, 1989), pp. 45–6

3   Otto Gelsted, 'Den Tyske Kulturs Sammenbrud' (The Collapse of German Culture), in *Aandehullet* (*The Breathing Hole*), vol. 1 (Copenhagen, 1933), p. 6

4   'De tilladte og de forbudte Badedragter' (The Permitted and the Forbidden Bathing Costumes), in *Københavnerinden* (*The Copenhagen Woman*) (Copenhagen, 11 November 1932)

5   Poul Henningsen, 'Du er selv Nazist' (You are a Nazi Yourself), in *Aandehullet* (*The Breathing Hole*), vol. I (Copenhagen, October 1933), p. 40

6   Poul Henningsen, *Hvad med Kulturen?* (*What About Culture?*) (Copenhagen, 1933), p. 44

7   'Den Store Buksemode' (The Great Trouser Fashion), in *Vore Damer og Ekko* (*Our Ladies and Echo*) (Copenhagen, 25 July 1930), p. 10

8 *Clearly Defined Female Forms c. 1947–64*

1 Article in *Tidens Kvinder* (*Modern Women*) (Copenhagen, 6 January 1948)
2 Article in *Nationaltidende* (*National Times*) (Copenhagen, 17 August 1954)
3 Article in *Berlingske Tidende* (Copenhagen, 9 October 1954)
4 R. Broby-Johansen, *Krop og Klær* (*Body and Clothes*) (Copenhagen, 1975), p. 223
5 R. Broby-Johansen, article in *Ekstrabladet* (*Extra Newssheet*) (Copenhagen, 30 November 1953)
6 R. Broby-Johansen, *Krop og Klær* (1975)
7 Simone de Beauvoir, *The Second Sex*, pp. 691–2
8 Barbara Sichtermann, *Weiblichkeit*

9 *Physical Desexualization c. 1965–78*

1 Rita Freedman, *Beauty Bound* (USA, 1986)
2 Article in *Berlingske Tidende* and *Aktuelt* (Copenhagen, 23 June 1964)
3 Article in *Berlingske Tidende* (Copenhagen, 23 June 1964)
4 Article in *Roskilde* (Roskilde, 9 July 1964)
5 Article in *Ekstrabladet* (Copenhagen, 23 June 1964)
6 Umberto Eco, 'Om at tænke med hofterne' (Thinking with the Hips), in *Middelalderens genkomst* (*The Return of the Middle Ages*) (Copenhagen, 1988), pp. 98–102
7 Betty Friedan, *The Second Stage* (Michael Joseph, 1982), p. 52
8 Articles removed from one context and then reorganized to communicate new meanings are called 'bricolage' – a term which was introduced into anthropology by Claude Lévi-Strauss and later used to describe subcultural style. *The Wild Thought* (Copenhagen, 1969)
9 Dick Hebdige, *Subculture: The Meaning of Style* (London, 1993), pp. 114–15

10 *New Physical Awareness and Greater Self-Confidence c. 1978–1990s*

1 Roland Barthes, *The Fashion System*
2 Jane Fonda, *Jane Fonda's Workout Book* (Workout Inc. in agreement with Lennart Sane Agency, 1981)
3 Linda Andersen, 'Pigeradikalitet eller tilpasning - om nødvendigheden af at sætte spor' (Radicality or Adjustment of Young Women – On the Necessity of Making Your Mark), in *Uddannelse* (*Education*), no. 5 (1988), pp. 282–8

Photographic Acknowledgements

Les Modes, March 1903, p. 2; photo George Hoyningen-Huené, p. 30; Danish National Museum, photo Roberto Fortuna, pp. 39, 85r; *Lady's Pictorial*, pp. 45, 89, 92t&b, 100, 103l; National Gallery, London, p. 46; Frederiksborg Castle, p. 48; Musée du Petit Palais, Paris, p. 49; photo Herb Ritts, p. 53b; Prado, Madrid, p. 59; Victoria and Albert Museum, London, p. 62; National Portrait Gallery, London, p. 63; photo Juncker-Jensen, 1900, p. 85l; *Journal des Desmoiselles*, p. 90l; *Nordisk Mønster-Tidende*, pp. 93, 95, 111l, 119, 143, 148l&r; *Dagmar*, p. 94l; *Les Modes*, pp. 94r, 106; photo Henri Mannes, p. 108; *Le Corset*, 1933, p. 111bl; *Vore Damer*, pp. 120, 121; *Politiken*, p. 129; *Harper's Bazaar*, pp. 130, 135, 136, 137, 145, 166, 169, 178; photo Hauerslev, p. 133; *Vogue*, pp. 53b, 149, 153, 180l, 186, 187, 190r, 198, 216; *Life*, p. 159; *Corset and Underwear Review*, pp. 160, 163, 165, 191; photo Willy Maxwald, p. 172; *Tidens Kvinder*, p. 173; photo David Bailey, *Vogue*, p. 180l; *Eva*, pp. 184t, 190l, 193b, 195, 197, 200, 208l&r, 209, 210; photo Richard Avedon, *Vogue*, p. 187; photo Asger Sessingø, p. 188; photo Lars Hansen, p. 196; *Muscle and Fitness*, p. 202r; *Elle*, pp. 214, 219l.

Index